AF443641

The Other

Thomas B. Smith

Establishment

An in-depth study of what individual life is really like in Communist-controlled countries

Regnery Gateway
Chicago

Published by Regnery Gateway, Inc.
360 West Superior Street
Chicago, Illinois 60610-0890

Manufactured in the United States of America

Library of Congress Cataloging in Publication Data

Smith, Thomas B., 1923–
  The other establishment

  Bibliography: p. 199
  Includes index.
  1. Identification cards—Law and legislation—Soviet Union. 2. Personality (Law)—Soviet Union. I. Title.
LAW   346.4701'2   83-63055
ISBN 0-89526-614-8   344.70612

NANCY

for patience, understanding
and sacrifice

ACKNOWLEDGEMENTS

This work owes whatever accuracy and consistency it possesses to the professional scrutiny of Dr. Ray Rocca.

Special thanks are due to the American Security Council Foundation and to Mr. John M. Fisher, without whom the work would not have seen publication in this form.

I am grateful also to those unnamed individuals in the Central Intelligence Agency who responded so precisely to my requests for document exemplars.

CONTENTS

INTRODUCTION

This book opens up to the American reader for the first time the grim world of Soviet control over the lives of ordinary people. That control is not maintained solely by the armed presence of the Red Army, Fleet and Air Force, but also by administrative devices which fortunately have no counterpart in our free society.

Western researchers have devoted considerable effort to examining the legal structure of the Soviet state, working with the overtly available publications which pass through the always controlled Soviet publishing channels. Unfortunately, most of their results are not easy reading, and mostly to be found only in academic libraries. Consequently, most Americans have had no detailed acquaintance with the legal system under which the Russian people must live.

It is generally recognized in the West that much of the language of the Soviet legal codes is pure propaganda, having little relation to the actual practice of law in the Soviet courts. It is cynical rhetoric, designed in part to gloss over the repressive true nature of

Marxism-Leninism. The problem for Western analysts is to separate this deliberate obfuscation from the essential intent and effect of the codes. In fact, it must be no easy matter for Soviet prosecutors and judges to square the humanism of some passages of the law with the inhumanity of Soviet reality. For example, some Western researchers have pointed out that a Soviet citizen can be convicted for an offense no more heinous than re-selling an item of clothing or a kitchen utensil.

Then there is the factor of police-state compulsion, with all its conspiratorial overtones, often operating quite at variance with the sometimes almost idealistic language of the legal codes. The KGB and MVD can blithely ignore the rules which theoretically govern investigations and civil rights.

There are some true gaps in Western scholarship on Soviet life, significant aspects of life under Communism which are virtually unknown here, even to specialists on the Soviet Union. One of these areas is the subject of this book, a critical slice of human life about which next to nothing has ever been written in the West. In the pages which follow the reader will see at first hand the institutions and devices used to regulate and regiment the everyday actions of every Soviet citizen. Through factual description and examples of real ID documents carried by real Soviet people, this work presents a clear picture of the police-state pressures which restrict everyday life, for *all* Soviets, not just the Dissidents or the doomed wretches in the *gulag* system.

The book relates this control-by-documents to the Soviet legal codes which back up the system, and details the registration procedures used by the police bureaucracy in carrying out these totalitarian rules.

The whole subject of control over individuals by a

system of personal identity documents, and the archival structure which stands behind it, are considered state secrets in the Soviet Union, as closely guarded as military planning, or nuclear capabilities. This is understandable, since any breakdown of this system of control over human beings could be as devastating to the maintenance of Marxist-Leninist order as the compromise of technical secrets. This is not the sort of topic a Soviet citizen discusses freely with Western visitors, so it is not surprising that only a handful of Americans, intelligence specialists, have ever had a real look inside this system. *The Other Establishment* is the first full-scale description in the West of this dark side of Marxism-Leninism in actual practice.

This unprecedented examination of Soviet identity control measures is forcefully illustrated by rare photos of the key papers themselves. These unique materials were obtained, in "sanitized" form, through the cooperation of the Central Intelligence Agency.

In *The Other Establishment* the reader becomes acquainted with the basic identity document which must be carried at all times by every Soviet person over sixteen. Its physical features, issuance, and uses are described in complete detail. Two chapters reveal how this documentary device can literally compel each citizen to live a life-style determined for him by the Communist state.

Succeeding chapters present the other key papers which govern all human activity in the Soviet Union—certifying military reserve status, Party membership, and employment and union affiliation. Special attention is given to labor supervision procedures which see to it that the individual is occupied in State-assigned, useful work throughout his (or her) productive life. All employment, time off work, all vacations and all pensions are controlled by the Communist Party through the *profsoyuz* apparatus in every workplace. Any Soviet citizen who consistently fights the Marxist-Leninist work ethic gets left out at vacation time, and upon retirement.

A section analyzes Soviet vital statistics documents—birth, death, marriage and divorce papers—and their procedures. These tools, so innocuous and useful in a free society, under Communism provide the glue which cements together the interlocking network of absolute state control over the individual, from the cradle to the grave.

A final chapter reveals the intimate connection between Soviet document controls and those used in the other countries of the "socialist commonwealth"; again, actual CIA photos of the basic ID papers used in those countries are presented and discussed.

The Other Establishment will be of particular interest to the specialist in Soviet law and to students of the Soviet Union in general. But beyond this, every citizen of the free world should be vitally concerned by the control system which it describes. All of us need to know of it, to decide for ourselves whether we are willing to support national policies which may one day bring to our shores a political system which so closely restricts the personal life of every last human.

1

What is it really like to live in the Soviet Union? Is life under a Communist regime, such as the Russian people have endured for over sixty years, really so different from what Americans know? Doesn't the average man get along pretty much the same in any country, regardless of the type of political system?

Many Americans have asked this question, if not publicly then at least of themselves. Indeed, it may become the most cogent political issue of our times. For some, attracted by the idealistic facade of theoretical Marxism, the answer is obvious. The Communist way, they say, is how all the world should and must live. But for most of us, even those who own little or no private property, an instinct warns us not to buy this political package. Even though we have never "been there," never had to experience Soviet reality at first hand, we feel that it is not for us.

Most Americans do not know, however, exactly why they feel this resistance. They realize that many Soviet citizens try to leave their homeland, and that plenty of others would do so if given the opportunity. Press coverage of dissidents and defectors shows that life is no bed of roses in an Iron Curtain country. But these people are special cases; the picture as it relates to the everyday life of the typical citizen is still unclear, lacking in convincing detail (except for the graphic description by Solzhenitsyn and the Dissidents of the lot of those Soviet citizens who fail to conform).

This book seeks to supply such detail, to show to American readers certain features of Soviet rule which set off life in the U.S.S.R. so drastically from the way most of us get along here, at any level of society.

Authoritarianism, like its opposite, democracy, is a relative thing, varying in degree from one autocratic country to another, from more or less benevolent despotism to absolute totalitarian rule. The extent of control over the life of individuals may be conditioned and limited by a variety of factors including deep-rooted traditions, the innate docility or intransigence of the population, geographic features, and linguistic and religious realities.

Given such considerations in smaller countries, we should logically expect that it would be difficult to install and maintain a thoroughly totalitarian regime in the vast, sprawling and non-homogeneous reaches of the Soviet Union. This colossus comprises one fifth of the land area of Earth, and includes scores of distinct racial and linguistic groups in its more than 240 million people. Add to this the fact that a majority of its citizens are of non-Great Russian heritage, minority peoples whose forebears were forcibly annexed to the Russian Empire before 1918 or to the Soviet Union since then. And even the Great Russian *Herrenvolk* themselves represent an unwilling, subjugated people. Once the most deeply religious of all Christians, they are now compelled by State policy to live an atheistic existence.

Nevertheless, after more than sixty years of Soviet rule the U.S.S.R. is one of the world's two most completely authoritarian societies, *and the model for all others*. It and Communist China are the most tightly controlled large social units the world has ever seen, and the first which can be called truly totalitarian. No previous ruler has been able to govern so large a population so absolutely as the Communist Parties of the U.S.S.R. and China. Our study will examine some of the devices which the Party elite have used to achieve this nearly airtight dominion over the diverse peoples of the Soviet Union. In the process we shall display facsimiles of materials used in this controls system and discuss their use.

A phenomenon which has undoubtedly aided the process of establishing control over the population is the uniquely Russian preoccupation with personal identity. Long before Lenin, determining and fixing exactly each human's identity *(lichnost')* was a distinctive feature of Russian culture, possibly associated with the xenophobic aspects of the Russian makeup noted by outsiders over many centuries of dealing with Russia. Since the time of the Tatar invasions, Russians have tended to distrust strangers, even from the next village, and local officials have concerned themselves with identifying each and every soul who belonged in their jurisdictions, and controlling the movements of any outsiders.

Personality is defined by the Great Soviet Encyclopedia as follows (italics supplied):

'only man, as a sensible being, with the power of speech *and the capability of labor activity,* is a per-

15

son. . . .No one is born into this world with completed characteristics, inclinations, etc. All these properties are developed and formed gradually, in the course of life. . .Innate *possibilities* become actual features of the person only as a result of the action of the surrounding medium on the child, under the controlling influence of rearing and training. . .a gigantic role in the development of the person is played by the *kollektiv*, especially in the conditions of the Soviet society. . ."[1]

These are viewpoints we might expect of a regime which sees human worth and progress solely in terms of group endeavor toward materialistic goals. In this system, inborn worth is no more than a "possibility," owing its ultimate attainments essentially to interaction with its environment. In other words, in the Communist state the outlines of the individual are shaped by the state (the *kollektiv*), since the latter can and does control that environment to whatever degree and extent it feels is necessary. And this control is aimed at insuring that the individual "person" is utilized in some activity deemed socially useful by Soviet standards, as we shall see in a detailed look at Soviet labor laws.

The Communists learned early in their history that the concept of exact pinpointing of a human being's *lichnost'* is critical in establishing real control over him. So, when they took power, far from abolishing the Tsars' practice of identifying free men by a system of identity documents, Lenin and his associates were astute enough to see that this device was precisely what the new dictatorship of the proletariat needed, if it was to regiment successfully the millions of Russians who had gotten rid of one set of autocratic masters in 1918, and were not anxious to see them replaced by new despots.

Soviet law distinguishes four distinct types of personal documents: 1) identity documents; 2) documents affirming a right or privilege; 3) papers which assert obligation or compulsion; and 4) documents which permit access to denied areas. Our analysis will omit categories two and four. Documents extending a right or privilege are pretty much common to all societies; a driver's license has no more political or social significance in the U.S.S.R. than in the U.S.A. Likewise, an access document, such as a badge of admission to a nuclear plant, has the same intent and effect in either society.

It is the first and third categories which epitomize the difference between the Communist state and our free culture. Except for the American's Social Security card there is no universal identity document for us, certainly none which specifies our residence and family background. Except for young men registered for possibly military draft, there exists for us no personal document which asserts an obligation to the State, or any other compulsion. But, as seen in the succeeding chapters, the Soviet citizen does indeed live with many compulsions, all of which are reflected tangibly in the papers which he must carry on his person.

The heart of the Soviet regime's system of control over the everyday actions of Soviet citizens is the device of identity documentation. The PASPORT system in its present evolved form makes it possible for governmental organs to identify unambiguously and instantly each of the 256 million Soviet citizens. But it is a device which does more than this. We shall also analyze the interlocking network of other personal documents and their registration, which have been developed in addition to the PASPORT, to reinforce and intensify the Party's control over each and every person.

This control concept has been scantily treated by Western researchers. Mention by them is limited to translations or paraphrases of overt data published in Soviet works. The chief Western analysis of the PASPORT system comprises three pages by Robert Conquest in *The Soviet Police System.*

Of course the Communists did not invent personal ID papers. Indeed this institution was already well entrenched in Russian society before 1918. The French word *passeport* is centuries old, implying a written permission to leave port. In pre-Communist Russia a document by this name was in use. As Harvard historian Richard Pipes has pointed out, it was introduced by Peter I as a means of enforcing the recruit levy. But it remained for the Bolsheviks to develop and perfect today's PASPORT system, which represents a combination of travel privilege, identity certification, and population control device. It is the culmination of generations of Tsarist autocracy, plus sixty-odd years of Communist effort toward total control over human life, a half century of experience in bringing diverse social groups under complete political, economic and ideological subjugation. It comes close to achieving complete regimentation of the vast body of Soviet peoples to a degree never dreamed of by the Tsars.

The device has enabled the Party to dispense with much of the naked armed might and overt Gestapo terror which earlier autocracies have found necessary to achieve anything like such domination. The Soviet system of control over the individual may lack the impact and drama of these cruder forms, but for effectiveness in the repression of the individual it surpasses any previous authoritarian method.

Some Western readers may find it difficult to accept the assertion that by merely issuing identity documents the Soviet government can regiment every aspect of life in an entire nation. In a sense they would be right of course. It is not the possession of a document that compels an individual to accept a life of regimentation. The real compulsion lies just out of sight, in the uniquely repressive Soviet legal codes, which can invoke what to us are inordinately severe consequences for the failure of a person to conform to the document regulations. The highly refined use of required personal documents and registration procedures is the lever which makes the codes operate at the human level. They are the point of contact where Marxist-Leninist dialectics bear directly on the realities of everyday human existence. Otherwise stated, the whole document control scheme works because the citizen must report to specific offices at specific times. If he does what is required, he does not run afoul of the legal codes, so the compulsive side of the system—namely the *militsiya* police, is not brought into play against him.

The codes spell out not only what is expected of or denied to the citizen in all areas of his life, but also specify what documents he must carry and how he will register them. Thus, in breaking some Marxist commandment he may well be punished not only for the transgression itself, but also for breach of the statute which describes the documentary procedure for correct conformity.

In the interest of fairness and perspective, it should be acknowledged that other countries have systems of identity documentation. Even some freeworld nations use *cartes d'identite* of one kind or another. For example, the Federal Republic of Germany has a close-knit system of residence registration not too different from the Soviet kind we shall be describing below, a survival of Germany's totalitarian past. The *Einwohnermeldeamt* in local German police stations functions in today's democratic state as a deterrent to crime and an aid in locating people, but in a less democratic framework it could offer a ready-made apparatus for repression.

Perhaps the most concise description of the Soviet PASPORT system is the following from the *Great Soviet Encyclopedia* under the entry *"pasportnaya sistema."*[2] It represents a condensed version of the actual language used in laws such as the *polozheniye o pasportakh:*

> The legal order of registration and regulation of the movement of the population. The PASPORT system presupposes the obligation of the citizen to have a PASPORT and to register it for residence. The PASPORT system was introduced...by the Council of People's Commissariats on 27 December 1932. It is governed by a special PASPORT regulation *(polozheniye o pasportakh)* (described in detail in the next chapter). In accordance with this regulation, all citizens on reaching sixteen are obliged to have PASPORTA. Here are listed the exceptions: persons on active military service, in hospitals or rest homes, or living in rural areas where the system is not in force.
>
> Within the confines of the area where the PASPORT system has been introduced, all citizens who change their place of residence, and also those arriving at a place for a period of over three

days, are obliged to yield their PASPORTA within 24 hours to officials responsible for registration. Persons leaving for a period of over 1½ months (except on official travel, vacation, medical treatment, to a *dacha*—vacation house, etc.), and persons changing residence within the confines of the same locality (changing quarters), persons called for active military service, persons sentenced to deprivation of freedom or to exile..., deceased persons (after registration of death),[3] are all subject to compulsory de-registration. Residence registration and de-registration are carried out with the House Book, according to a prescribed form.[4] Breaking the rules of the PASPORT system subjects one to administrative or criminal responsibility.[5] The PASPORT system is not extended to foreigners living in the U.S.S.R., nor to stateless persons.

The Soviet PASPORT, which is illustrated by photographs of all pages in the next chapter, is the jewel in the crown of the Soviet hierarchy of personal documentation, and a document which every thinking American should examine with interest and attention. This is no Master Charge or Diner's Club card. Its text makes no mention of any rights or privileges, only obligations and threats of punishment for failure to live up to them. And foremost among these obligations is, as quoted above, the absolute compulsion for everyone to have and always carry such a document.

But any Soviet citizen without a PASPORT is in even worse shape. By definition he is either on active military service, in penal servitude, or physically or mentally unfit to be among his fellow citizens. From the viewpoint that by holding a PASPORT a Soviet citizen is able to live a "normal" life and to move about from one place to another if he follows the prescribed registration procedures, he may be considered privileged. Of course by our standards he pays a high price for the privilege. He must produce his PASPORT upon demand of any official who says to him: *"Vashe bumagi!"* ("Your papers!") From a quick look at the PASPORT an official can see nearly everything but the immortal soul of the person standing before him, because its entries contain information representing an invasion of personal privacy which would be regarded as intolerable in the free world.

Until now there has existed a very large category of Soviet inhabitants who lived out their lives without the dubious benefits of the PASPORT system. These are the millions of collective farm workers *(kolkhozniki)*, who live in rural areas and work primarily on State-owned lands. In order to keep these people in place, to prevent their flight to the cities in search of a more human existence, the Soviet regime has denied them PASPORTA through all the half century of "building the Communist state." Without a PASPORT the *kolkhoznik* has been unable legally to leave his assigned village, unable to obtain a *komandirovka* (travel document) or *spravka* release paper, or even to buy a train ticket. He has been bound to the land just as effectively as was the serf under the Tsars' feudal *krepostnaya* system prior to 1861. The denial of the PASPORT has literally made a modern-day slave of the *kolkhoznik*, far worse off than his pasportized countrymen in the towns in terms of personal and economic freedom.

Fortunately for the *kolkhozniki* this situation has begun to change. European observers began to report as early as 1976 that the Soviet government was planning to include the collective farmers in the PASPORT system. The stimulus for this radical change is unclear. It may be that overcrowding in urban areas had begun to make moving to the city less attractive, or possibly the rural population may have reached a point where scarcity of farm labor is no longer a problem. Or this move may simply have been a part of the major change in the format of the PASPORT (described in detail in Chapter 2) which likewise began to be manifested from 1976. Whatever the reason, the central archives systems must now be swelled by data on millions of rural Soviet citizens whose records previously had been a matter of purely local concern. From now on, in theory, *any* Russian will be able to go elsewhere in his own land, if he has the price of a ticket, and if he faithfully follows the strict rules of registration and deregistration which we shall describe below.

In the next chapter we shall examine the PASPORT booklet itself and the entries it contains. Keep in mind that if indeed Marxism is the wave of the future, we shall also one day be carrying such a document—in an English-language edition of course.

FOOTNOTES

1. *Bol'shaya Sovetskaya Entsiklopediya*, 1st ed., Moscow vol. 25, p. 304.
2. Ibid., vol. 32, p. 200.
3. See Chapter Six, "ZAGS".
4. See discussion of the House Book in Chapter Two.
5. "Administrative responsibility" refers to punishment by *militsiya* officials, without court trial.

2

The Soviet citizen's basic identity document called "PASPORT" exists in a Russian-language-only edition used *throughout the Russian Soviet Federated Socialist Republic (R.S.F.S.R.) and in two-language versions in other constituent Soviet republics.* This statement may come as a surprise to some Western scholars, who recognized the PASPORT system in force only in certain limited areas of the Soviet Union. Thus, even Conquest, writing in 1968, describes the extent of *pasportization* as follows:

Under the 'Regulation Concerning PASPORTS' approved by the U.S.S.R. Council of Ministers on October 21, 1953, 'all citizens over 16 permanently living in towns, *raion* centres, inhabited points where the passport system is in force, and in all inhabited points of the forbidden zones and frontier strips, are obliged to possess internal passports issued by the Militia. The passport system is also in force throughout the three Baltic Republics and the Moscow *oblast,* and in many *raions* of the Leningrad *oblast.*[1]

The writer can state from first-hand experience with the original documents themselves and the people who carried them that the system has been in effect in all the Soviet republics, at least as far back as World War II. Captured German intelligence files (of the *Fremde Heere Ost*) contain literally hundreds of exemplars of PASPORTA seized by German forces in various regions of the country other than the R.S.F.S.R. and the Baltic. Further, Article 198 of the Criminal Code states unequivocally, "...the PASPORT system is in effect in the entire territory of the U.S.S.R."

The pre-1976 PASPORT itself is a booklet about 8×11 centimeters, bound together with two wire staples. In the Russian-only version it contains fourteen text pages; the two-language editions have extra pages which duplicate pages 1, 2 and 3 in the second language, and also the final page which contains extracts of the PASPORT regulations. In the remaining pages, those for "special remarks" (*osobyye otmetki*) and "residence registration" (*propiska*), the versions differ only in that the two-language types contain these words in the native language side by side with the Russian headings. (See Figures 1–5.)

The Soviet pre-1976 PASPORT is one of the world's most technically complex and expensive printing efforts, comparable to the most sophisticated banknote production in any country. In the first place, the paper stock of the pages has a particular waffle-design watermark which is employed exclusively for this booklet and a few other critical personal documents. By simply holding a page up to the light a *militsiya* officer can check the authenticity of the material.

Next come several printing features which, taken together, make U.S. currency printing seem almost casual. Initially the watermarked paper stock is "underprinted" with a scarcely noticeable fine design of overlapping sine curves in pale olive green, much like security check printing in this country. Any attempt at erasure of entries cause this pattern to come off and be unmistakably apparent.

On the PASPORT a special multi-colored process is used to print a design vertically down the middle of the first three pages of the Russian-only version, in pale pastel colors which fuse from pink to salmon to blue, and then repeat. Over this image is then printed, in light brownish ink, the word "PASPORT" in large, very fancy shaded art letters. (See Figure 1.)

The separate text printing for all entries and instructions is in black ink. It is distinctive only in having somewhat stylized Cyrillic characters, just different enough from ordinary Russian book printing to make substitution or reproduction difficult, requiring expensive art-work and plate-making.

The remaining technical features and controls in the PASPORT will be discussed as we investigate the individual entries in order.

At the top of this page, in all editions, is printed the great seal of the U.S.S.R. and the word "PASPORT" in Russian. Immediately below this is an unnumbered entry reading "valid until...". The day and month entered here always correspond exactly to those entered on the next page under "Date of issuance...," but the year in the former entry depends on the age status of the bearer.

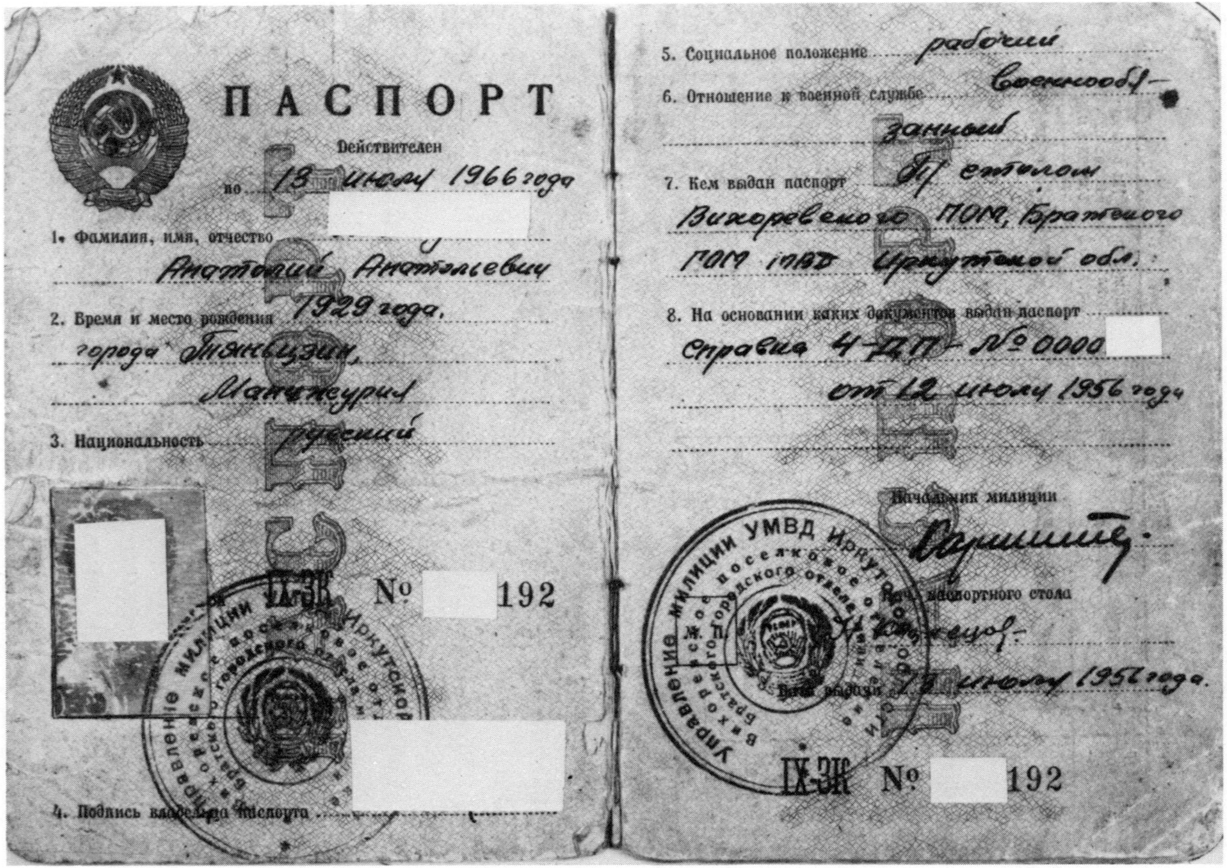
ПАСПОРТ

Действителен

по 13 июля 1966 года

1. Фамилия, имя, отчество

Анатолий Анатольевич

2. Время и место рождения 1929 года,

города Тяньцзин,

Маньчжурия

3. Национальность русский

IX-ЗК № 192

4. Подпись владельца паспорта

5. Социальное положение рабочий

6. Отношение к военной службе Военнообя-

занный

7. Кем выдан паспорт П/столом

Вихоревского ПОМ, Братского

ГОМ УМВД Иркутской обл.

8. На основании каких документов выдан паспорт

Справка 4-ДП № 0000

от 12 июля 1956 года

Начальник милиции

Нач. паспортного стола

Дата выдачи 13 июля 1956 года.

Управление милиции УМВД Иркутской обл. Вихоревское поселковое отделение милиции Братского городского отдела милиции

IX-ЗК № 192

Figure 1

The intent of the Soviet government upon setting up the PASPORT system can be seen from the official description of the validity structure given in the *Great Soviet Encyclopedia:*

> Four types of PASPORT have been established: of unlimited validity for persons who have attained forty years of age; ten-year PASPORTA for persons of age twenty to forty; five-year PASPORTA for persons aged sixteen to twenty; and short-term PASPORTA, for periods not over six months.[2]

In practice this scheme was not followed in many respects, probably due to the disruption to Soviet civil order caused by World War II. During the war years some citizens received a one-sheet temporary identity document entitled VREMENNOYE UDOSTOVERENIYE, printed on watermarked PASPORT paper and usually valid either for six months, or for one year (referred to as *pasport na odin god*). The need for the authorities to maintain a stricter, more frequent control over identity documents probably was also the reason why no PASPORT of ten years or unlimited validity was ever seen by Western intelligence observers until the early 1950s. Both of these types are now common, so current practice now seems to coincide with the originally planned concept of PASPORT validity.

Numbered entry 1 calls for the family name, first name and patronymic of the bearer. In practice the fill-in invariably follows that order, with the family name on the first line, and the first name and patronymic on the line below. The patronymic is never omitted, even in those republics where non-Russian and even non-Indo-European language names predominate. Thus, in the republic of Georgia, the patronymic consists of the father's name plus "-ovich" (-evich) on the Russian language page, but the name plus the Georgian familial suffix "-dze" on the corresponding Georgian-language page. Similarly in Azerbaydzhan, on the Turkish-language page we see the father's name plus "-oglu."

Entry 2 calls for the bearer's birth date and place. In the illustrated exemplar only the birth year appears, probably because the bearer was born outside the U.S.S.R., in Manchuria, and exact birth data may not have been at hand. This is most uncommon; the writer can recall no postwar examplar other than this one in which day and month of birth did not appear here. On the following two lines are given, in prescribed order, the city (or town or village) of birth, then the *raion*, then the *oblast'* or region or republic.

Entry 3 calls for the nationality of the bearer; that is, his ethnic origin, not his citizenship (*grazhdanstvo* in Russian). In our society this entry would be considered an infringement of the bearer's civil liberties, a source of ethnic discrimination. By a glance at this entry an official can know the true ethnic background of the person standing before him, regardless of how his name is spelled, or what he looks like. In a land where the "Great Russian" controls the establishment, a person who has any entry other than "*russkiy*" ("Great Russian") in this category is automatically subject to some discrimination. This discrimination may be conscious or unwitting, and may vary in degree according to the ethnic group concerned. But clearly the word "*yevrey*" ("Jew") or "*tsigan*" ("gypsy") in one's PASPORT will pose serious obstacles to success in many fields. To find counterparts to this ugly example of ethnic discrimination we must look back to the "pale" system of the Tsars, or to the *"Ausrottung"* policy of the Nazis, or to South African apartheid in today's world.

The writer can recall the following ethnic designations cited in actual PASPORTA. This listing is alphabetical, not in order of their frequency of occurrence; indeed some entries apply to only a few thousand individuals.

1. abkhazets = Abkhazian
2. adzhar = Moslem Georgian
3. azerbaydzhanets = Azerbaijanian
4. aysor = "Assyrian"
5. armyanin = Armenian
6. balkar = Balkar
7. beloruss = White Russian
8. finn = Finn
9. gruzin = Georgian
10. yevrey = Jew
11. kabardin = Kabardino Cherkessian
12. kazakh = Kazakh
13. kirgiz = Kirgiz
14. krimtatar = Crimean Tatar
15. kurd = Kurdish
16. latviyskiy = Latvian
17. litovets = Lithuanian
18. moldavan = Moldavian
19. osetin = Ossetian
20. mordvin = Mordvinian
21. russkiy = Russian
22. tadzhik = Tadjik
23. tatar = Tatar
24. tyurk = Turkmen
25. ukrainets = Ukrainian
26. uzbek = Uzbek
27. tsygan = gypsy
28. cherkess = Adygei Cherkessian

This is by no means a complete listing of Soviet nationalities as used in the PASPORT, but merely those the writer recalls having seen in Entry 3. It should be noted that all the above ethnic names are in masculine form, and that for each of these there is a corresponding feminine version used in the PASPORTA of women.

Entry 4 calls for the signature of the bearer.

The remaining features of the first page of the PASPORT are essentially measures designed to prevent misuse or falsification. At the lower left is glued a full-face bust photo (never profile) of the bearer. Over the lower left corner of the photo is impressed a small circular "dry seal," made by a metal die similar to those used by notaries in this country. This contains the simple text "MGB SSSR" (or "MVD," or whatever ministry-level organ the *militsiya* was subordinate to at the time of issue).

Partially covering the lower right corner is always seen a somewhat larger circular stamped cachet in ink (usually purplish or blue-purple, except in some non-Russian areas). This stamp contains one or more rings of text which cite the *militsiya* precinct which issued the document. Enclosed within the text ring(s) is the *gerb* (great seal), in this instance of the R.S.F.S.R., with its wheat sheaves, hammer and sickle, and republic banner.

The other control feature on this page is the PASPORT serial. Its purpose is to aid in identification and thwart falsification, which is accomplishes quite effectively through the complex coding of the serial elements.

Let us consider a theoretical PASPORT with complete serial XX SU No. 677542 printed in it. To the average Soviet citizen the number would have little meaning, but to any police official who knows the system it tells a great deal. Without reading further he can see that the document was issued in Moscow *oblast'* because of the SU prefix, and that it must have been issued in the early 1950's (from the size of the Roman-numeral element; and because more recently the letters SA have replaced the original SU pair). If the handwritten issuance data on pages one and two do not bear out these observations, the official knows he is dealing with a falsification.

The PASPORT shown in Figure 1 bears the Cyrillic prefix ZK, which signifies Irkutsk *oblast'*. This is borne out by the entry data in Item 7.

As a further measure against forgery, a serial number is printed in seven different places in the PASPORT (Russian version), located in such a way that every page-spread in the stapled booklet shows the serial at least once, on one side of the sheet. This makes it next to impossible to insert false pages without printing on them an exact duplication of the original serial number. So, in our PASPORT illustration we see the serial number appearing on pages 1, 2, 4, 7, 8, 11 and 13. (See Figures 1-4.)

Entry 5 has the title "social position." This is another category which would be regarded in the free world as an infringement of the bearer's rights, with discriminatory implications. Indeed, this entry, which is invariably filled in with a single laconic word, symbolizes the essential difference between the free world and the Marxist-Leninist society. Every Soviet citizen over sixteen must be officially designated here as belonging to one or another of the few legally defined categories, which basically describe the bearer's usefulness to society. Analysis of many PASPORTA shows the following categories in use:

1. *rabochiy* = "worker" (or "factory worker"). Probably more Soviet citizens bear this notation in their PASPORTA than any other.

2. *sluzhashchiy* = "employee" (or "white-collar worker," or "civil servant"). Considering the enormous bureaucratic edifice which Communism requires, this category also includes a large chunk of the *pasportized* population.

3. *krestyanin* (sometimes *krestyanin-yedinolichnik*)= "peasant," or "individual farmer." This entry is seen mostly in those areas which are unsuited to collective farming.
4. *kolkhoznik* = "collective farm worker." Until now few such persons have been included in the PAS-PORT system, as mentioned in Chapter One. If the government does carry out the reported *pasportization* of *kolkhozniki,* such people would represent a substantial portion of the Soviet population.
5. *uchashchisya* = "student," in universities and other institutions of higher learning, and those over sixteen who are still in middle school.
6. *pensioner'* = "retired person."
7. *izhdivenets* = "dependent." This entry is used in the PASPORTA of persons who do not fit any of the above work categories, for whatever reason. The word is usually followed by the social status of the person in the family upon whom the bearer is dependent. For example, *"izhdivenka sluzhashchego"* signifies the woman dependent of a white-collar worker.

The bearer himself has no say as to the type of entry made for him under Item 5. This has been predetermined by his age, education, I.Q., work background, accomplishments, etc., as of the date the PASPORT was issued, and the PASPORT desk official in the *militsiya* precinct decides the wording of the entry. It is not an exaggeration to say that this entry validates a caste element which undeniably exists in the vaunted "classless society" of the Soviet Union, since only persons in the *"sluzhashchiy"* category have any real chance to advance beyond the most routine and unrewarding existence.

Entry 6 is entitled "bearer's relationship to military service." The only notations entered here are either "*voyennoobyazannyy*" (" liable for military service"), or "*ne voyennoobyazannyy*" for persons not subject to conscription, for whatever reason. As we'll see in a subsequent chapter on the military service booklet, this entry is superfluous, since all males must carry the latter document on the person until age 55, just as they must carry the PASPORT. Further, the military service booklet shows the bearer's draft status and background in complete detail. This overlapping of functions in Soviet personal documents is a characteristic of the whole controls system; we shall see numerous examples of such duplication of effort. Obviously the regime prefers to err on the side of thoroughness, rather than let one individual escape his social responsibilities through lack of adequate checking on him.

Entry 7 is entitled "by whom the PASPORT was issued." The fill-in of this entry follows a strict formula: "by the PASPORT desk of so-and-so *militsiya* section, MGB (or MVD, etc.), of so-and-so *oblast'*." In our illustrated document we see the text: "by the Vikhorevskiy settlement *militsiya* section, Bratsk city *militsiya* section, MVD, of Irkutsk *oblast'*."

Entry 8 reads "on the basis of which documents the PASPORT was issued." This may seem an unnecessary item, but in the Soviet Union, with its emphasis on control over the individual, this feature has real importance. Citing the basis of issue provides other officials with a means of checking authenticity and knowing where to seek additional data on suspect persons.

Most Soviet citizens over twenty will have an entry here which cites a previous PASPORT serial number; younger persons will usually have a birth certificate number and the ZAGS (vital statistics registry) office which issued it.[3] However, in exceptional cases other entries may be observed here. Indeed, our illustrated exemplar shows an unusual entry for Item 8. It cites an unspecified certificate as basis of issue. The cryptic nature of this entry, with its two-letter prefix and complete omission of the issuing organ, makes it likely that the bearer was either just released from incarceration, exile, or other nonpasportized status, or had been repatriated. The last seems likely, because of the bearer's age (about 27), and the fact that the vague *spravka* certificate was issued only one day prior to the issue date of the PASPORT itself.

The writer has seen other entries in this heading which cited an article of the PASPORT regulation (*polozheniye o pasportakh*) as basis of issue. Only insiders, such as *militsiya* officials, would understand the exact meaning of such entries.

The remaining features of the second page are the signatures of the *militsiya* chief (*nachal'nik militsii*) and the PASPORT desk chief (*nachal'nik pasportnogo stola*), and the date of issue. The same circular rubber stamp used for page 1 is also stamped here, covering a small rectangle ("place for stamp") and validating the signature.

In the two-language PASPORTA used in the other fourteen Soviet republics, the first two pages which we have just examined are exactly duplicated, but this time with all text printing and (usually) the handwritten fill-in in the republic language rather than Russian. The Cyrillic alphabet, with some modifications, is used for all these languages except Georgian, Armenian, and the three Baltic tongues (Latvian, Lithuanian, and Estonian). The validating cachets in most cases have alternating rings of text in Russian and the republic language, and are used for all four pages.

Page Three of the PASPORT contains entry 9, which occupies the entire page and has space for ten children of the bearer. The entry title reads "persons entered in the bearer's PASPORT," but in actual practice this page is used exclusively for children under sixteen. The entry calls for the full name of the child, with patronymic, its age, relationship to the bearer, and the documentary basis for being so registered, and by whom. In the illustrated example we note a daughter, born 9 July 1957, and the documentary basis is a numbered vital statistics paper, with the general title "*Akt.*" This again is an unusual entry; ordinarily a birth certificate number would be cited here. The entry is validated by a signature, presumably of an official of ZAGS, the vital statistics organ. (See Figure 2.)

All of the handwritten data entered on the three pages discussed so far are normally entered by the PASPORT desk official, or someone in his office who possesses a suitably legible hand. Some of the writing seen in PASPORTA borders on calligraphy. All the entries are made invariably in a special heavy black waterproof ink *(tush')*, which is not normally available to the average Soviet citizen.

The next three pages of the PASPORT are essentially blank sheets, except for the heading "special remarks" at the top. These remarks fall into one of three main types of control data.

Most important of these categories, and the one which is pertinent to all working persons, is the certification of employment. This takes the form of rectangular stamped cachets showing hiring and release from employment. Whenever a Soviet citizen is taken on in

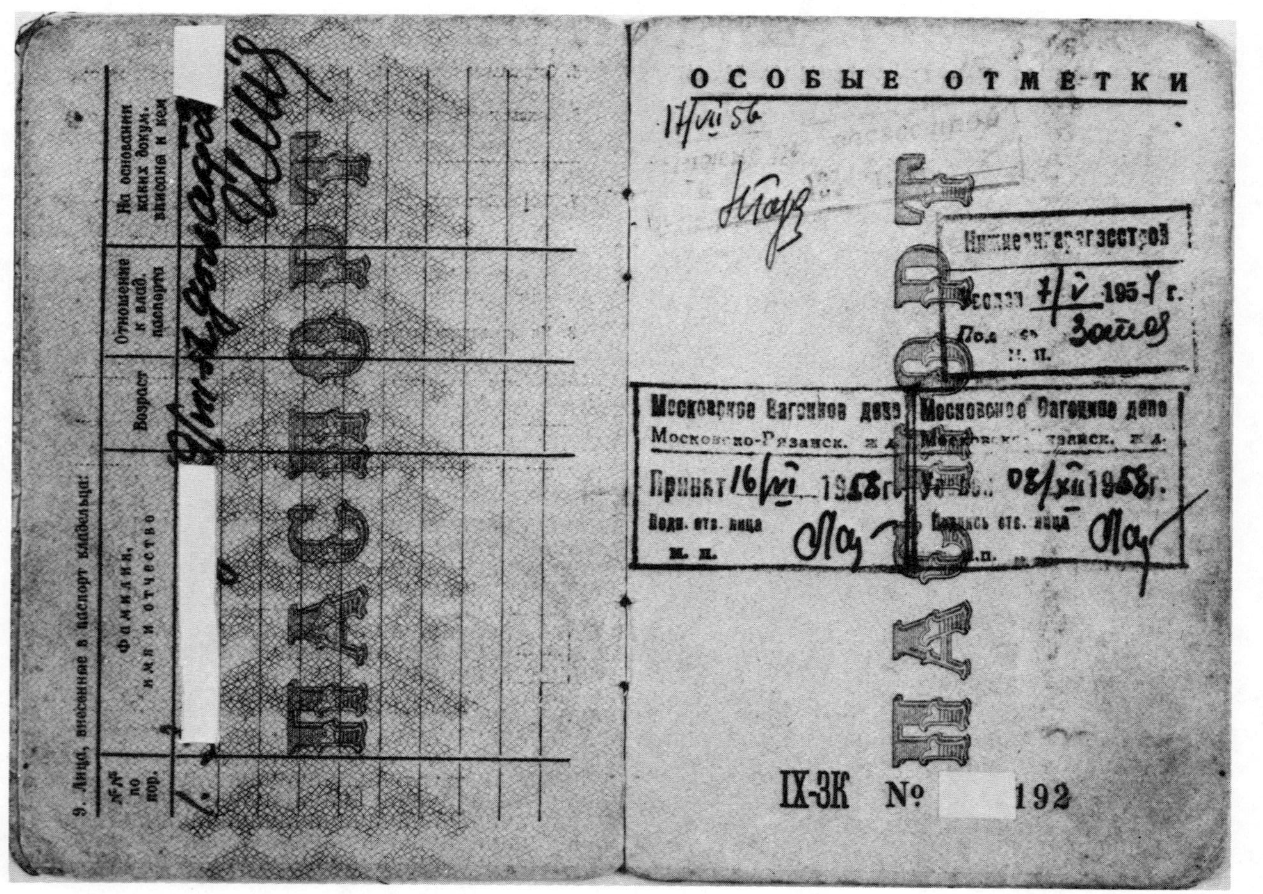

9. Лица, внесенные в паспорт владельца:
№№ по пор.
Фамилия, имя и отчество
Возраст
Отношение к влад. паспорта
На основании каких докум. внесена и кем
ПАСПОРТ
ОСОБЫЕ ОТМЕТКИ
Нишнечнтаргизсстрой
Весели 7/V 195 г.
Под. Зайцев
м. п.
Московское Вагонное депо
Московско-Рязанск. ж.д.
Принят 16/VI 1958 г.
Подп. отв. лица
м. п.
Московское Вагонное депо
Московско-Рязанск. ж.д.
05/XII 1958 г.
Подпись отв. лица
м. п.
ПАСПОРТ
IX-ЗК № 192

Figure 2

any kind of employment (which virtually by definition is in a State-run enterprise), the personnel office of the organization enters an inked stamp of this kind, affirming that the bearer was hired on such and such date. In the event the bearer should leave that employment, a similar cachet is stamped beside or below it, stating that he was released on that date. (Note that the Russian word is "released" (uvolen), a semantically illuminating indication that the individual does not really terminate employment at his own volition. We shall pursue this topic in detail in the chapter on the Work Booklet.) If this release cachet is not present, the bearer cannot be legally hired anywhere else in the U.S.S.R., because the last entry still shows him as employed at the previous organization.

This system of controls is another example of redundancy. Far more detailed information on the individual's hiring, work record, and release is contained in his Work Booklet *(TRUDOVAYA KNIZHKA)*, another personal document owned by every working Soviet citizen. It is another indication of the omnipresence and power of the *militsiya* police. The legal basis for this entering of work data in the PASPORT is unclear; both the Criminal and Labor Codes are explicit about the requirement of proper registration for employment and release in the Work Booklet, but there is no mention of simultaneous entering of such data in the PASPORT. It seems likely that this topic is covered by passages of the *polozheniye o pasportakh* not available in the West.

The Work Booklet is described and illustrated in detail in Chapter Four.

In Figure 2 we see page four of our sample PASPORT, containing two hiring and two release cachets. The first set is from the construction organization of the Lower Angara River hydro-electric station, the second from the Moscow Car Depot of the Moscow-Ryazan Railway. Each stamp is signed by the "responsible person," which is to say an official of the personnel section (*otdel kadrov*) of the organization. Most employment cachets, like those illustrated, contain the letters "*m.p.*", which call for circular validating stamps which every Soviet enterprise possesses. However, in actual practice this feature seems to be largely ignored.

The second chief use of the "Special Remarks" pages is to record data on marriage and divorce. This is a further invasion of the individual's privacy. Such entries in one's PASPORT make it difficult for him to keep to himself details of his marital past from anyone who may get a look at his PASPORT, such as a new girl-friend.

The marriage cachet used by city *raion* ZAGS offices is a long flat rectangle nearly twice the size of an employment stamp. The text reads, "*ZAREGISTRIROVAN V BRAKE*" = "registered in marriage," followed by a space for the name of the spouse. A Russian wife may legally use either her maiden name or her husband's family name, but the maiden name must be cited in this entry.

Our sample PASPORT contains a marriage entry (see Figure 3), but this is handwritten, probably because it was issued by a village council (*sel'sovet*) in Irkutsk oblast, Siberia. The entry is validated instead with the round cachet of the council.

Divorce is recorded in the PASPORT also, by entering a rectangular cachet similar to the marriage stamp except for the word "*razvod*" (divorce). If a wife upon divorce wishes to resume use of her former name, an

Figure 3

entry must be made in the PASPORT by ZAGS, alerting *militsiya* officials to the fact that she must apply for a new PASPORT in that name.

Explicit instructions for concerned officials from all organizations are contained in the *grazhdanskiy protsessual'nyy kodeks RSFSR* (Civil Trial Code of the R.S.F.S.R.). According to these regulations, marriage and divorce cachets are to be entered not only in the PASPORT, but also stamped onto the person's birth certificate and, for military personnel, into the officer's identity book *(UDOSTOVERENIYE LICHNOSTI OFIT-SERA)* or enlisted man's booklet *(SLUZHEBNAYA KNISHKA)*, "...on the first blank page." This creates an interlocking network of controls, whereby officials not only of the ZAGS vital statistics organization, but also from various other ministry subordinations, know the exact family status of each individual with whom they come into contact. All of these notations are of course redundant, since the basic legal registration of marriage and divorce consists of the marriage and divorce certificates issued by ZAGS. These are treated in greater detail in the chapter on ZAGS.

The "Special Remarks" pages of the PASPORT are reserved and intended for one further type of population control, this one over movement and residence of persons entering or residing in 1) a Soviet border strip *(pogranichnaya polosa)*, or 2) a border zone *(pogranichnaya zona)*. Probably the most recent definitions of these two sensitive areas are the following concerning Article 197 of the Criminal Code, extracted from a Regulation Concerning Guarding of the State Borders of the U.S.S.R., affirmed by the Presidium of the Supreme Soviet of the U.S.S.R., dated 5 August 1960:

The border strip is established separately for each section of the border. As a rule it does not exceed 2 km from the State border, on dry land, or from the banks of rivers or lakes. The border zones are established, as a rule, as the confines of the territories of *raion*, city or settlement Councils adjacent to State borders. Included also are territorial and internal sea waters of the U.S.S.R. and the Soviet portion of border rivers and lakes.

In observed practice the depth of the border zone seems not to exceed about twenty kilometers.

Any Soviet citizen authorized to live in either of these two specially controlled border areas must have a cachet stamped into his PASPORT on one of the "Special Remarks" pages, to prove this authorization. Our sample PASPORT does not contain such a stamp; however, in the Hungarian basic identity document (SZEMELYI IGAZOLVANY) illustrated in Chapter Eight, we are privileged to see an almost exact duplicate of the large cachet used for the Soviet border zone. Like this Hungarian copy the Russian stamp has ornamented edges and a large numeral 2 at the right side. It is perhaps worth noting that the text of the Russian cachet reads, "zhitel' zapretnoy zony" (inhabitant of a *forbidden* zone), rather than of a "border" zone as described in the law. Inhabitants of the two kilometer border strip have similar large cachets in the PASPORT, differing only in having a large numeral 1 instead of the 2 used for the border zone. Soviet border cachets also contain small Cyrillic letter pairs (not seen in the Hungarian version); these are obviously part of a code system to aid in detecting violations of the border areas.

П Р О П И С К А   П Р О П И С К А

ИРКУТСКАЯ ОБЛАСТЬ
Вихоревское поселковое отделение милиции
Братского района
ПРОПИСАН ПОСТОЯННО
по ул.
195 г.

ИРКУТСКАЯ ОБЛАСТЬ
Вихоревское поселковое отделение милиции
района
ВЫПИСАН
1957 г.

18 г. МОСКВА
отдел. Милиции
ПРОПИСАН ПОСТОЯННО

18 г. МОСКВА
отдел. Милиции

18 г. МОСКВА
отдел. Милиции

IX-ЗК № 192

IX-ЗК № 192

Figure 4

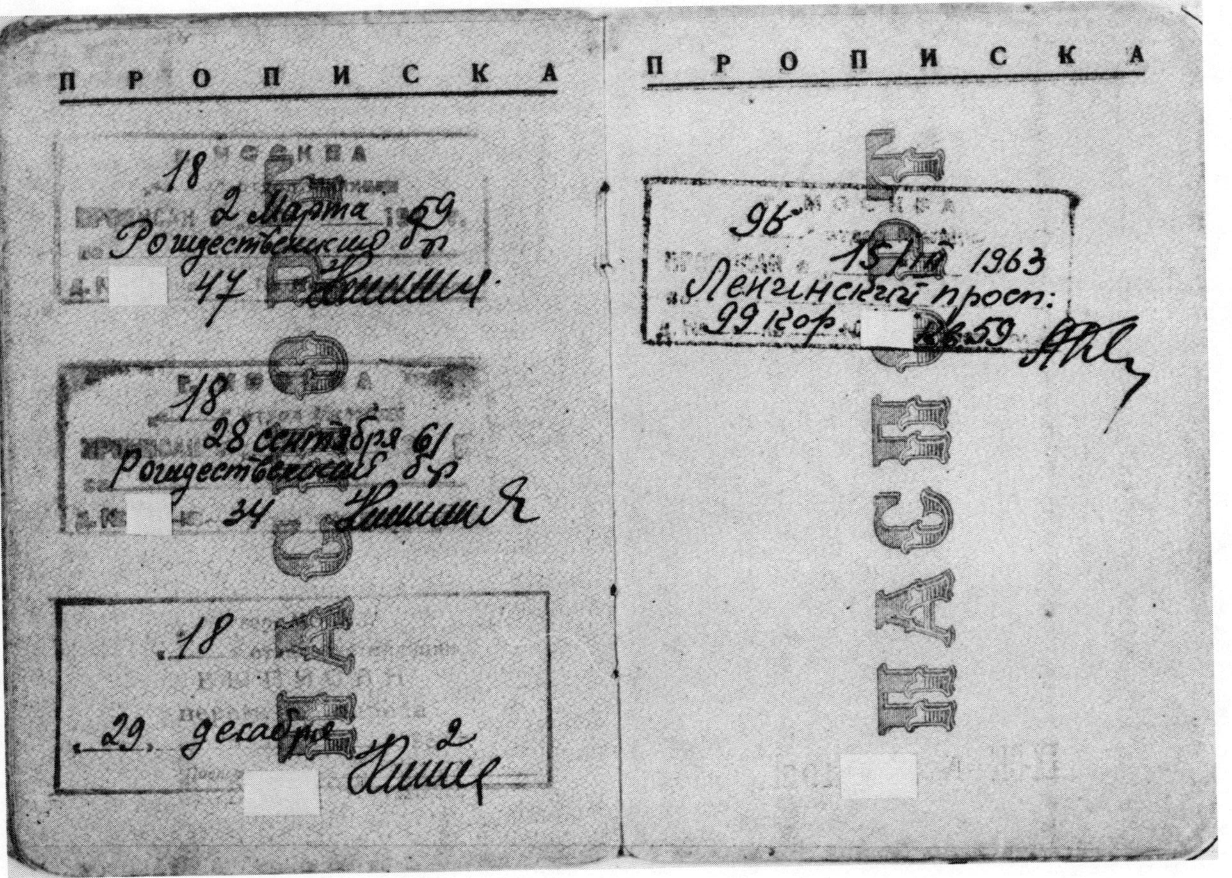

Figure 4 continued

No persons except those whose PASPORTA contain these special cachets are permitted to enter or reside for any time whatsoever in either of the two border areas, except with the approval of the M.V.D. This approval takes the form of a special pass *(PROPUSK)* which is printed on "Goznak" watermarked and underprinted paper. This entry document is used only after the MVD has conducted an investigation of the person who requests entry into the zone. Any unauthorized entry into the areas incurs punishment under Article 197 of the R.S.F.S.R. Criminal Code.

Following the "Special Remarks" pages in the PASPORT come seven more, likewise largely blank pages, with the heading *"PROPISKA"* ("residence registration"). We shall put off discussion of the entries made under this heading, since this is a topic which deserves treatment in a full chapter.

The final printed page in the PASPORT is a glued-down page which forms the inside back cover. In the more recent printings of the PASPORT, beginning about 1952, this page has been used to carry instructions on the use of the PASPORT and the obligations of its holders. In previous editions this page had always been left blank, except for the word "Goznak" and the printing year at the bottom.

As seen in Figure 5, this page consists of extracts from the *polozheniye o pasportakh* of 21 October 1953. As a matter of fact, this page represents the only overt published text of that special piece of legal foundation which the writer has seen. The page cites ten Articles, of which the highest numbered is Article 38. We have no way of knowing the total number of articles in the *polozheniye.*

Because of the critical importance of these regula-

П Р О П И С К А

ПАСПОРТ

IX-ЗК № 192

И З В Л Е Ч Е Н И Я

из Положения о паспортах, утвержденного Постановлением
Совета Министров СССР от 21 октября 1953 года

Ст. 1. Граждане СССР в возрасте от 16 лет и старше, проживающие в городах, районных центрах, поселках городского типа,... обязаны иметь паспорта.

Ст. 7. Паспорта выдаются органами милиции по месту жительства граждан.

Ст. 12. Паспорта подлежат обмену в случаях: а) истечения срока действия; б) изменения фамилии или имени; в) обнаружения неточностей в записях; г) негодности для пользования...

Ст. 13. В случаях утери или хищения паспорта владелец его обязан немедленно заявить об этом письменно в орган милиции по месту жительства или пребывания...

Ст. 14. ...Изъятие, прием и передача паспорта в качестве залога запрещается...

Ст. 15. Граждане, прибывающие на жительство из одной местности в другую на срок свыше трех суток, переменившие жилую площадь в пределах одного и того же населенного пункта, получившие паспорта вновь или обменявшие их, обязаны в суточный срок сдать свои паспорта... лицам, ответственным за прописку, для представления в органа милиции на прописку...

Ст. 22. Не разрешается прописка лиц, прибывших на постоянное жительство, если в их паспортах нет отметки о выписке с прежнего места жительства...

Ст. 25. Лица, прибывшие в командировку, отпуск, на лечение или на дачу в период летнего сезона, прописываются без отметок в паспортах о выписке.

Ст. 37. Граждане СССР, обязанные в соответствии со статьей 1 настоящего Положения иметь паспорта, за проживание без паспорта или с просроченным паспортом, а также без прописки подвергаются в административном порядке штрафу... Этой же ответственности подвергаются граждане, утерявшие паспорта.

Ст. 38. Повторное нарушение гражданами СССР установленных правил прописки паспортов влечет за собой уголовную ответственность... Проживание без паспортов лиц, обязанных иметь их по закону и подвергавшихся ранее административному взысканию за это нарушение, влечет за собой уголовную ответственность...

Гознак. 1954.

Figure 5

tions for the political and social life of every Soviet citizen (and the wider implications of their possible spread to all areas of Marxist-Leninist influence), we shall present here a translation of those Articles cited in the PASPORT:

Article 1. Citizens of the U.S.S.R. of 16 years and older, living in cities, *raion* centers, city-type settlements...are required to have PASPORTA.

Article 7. PASPORTA are issued by organs of the *militsiya* at the place of residence of the citizens.

Article 12. PASPORTA are subject to replacement in cases: a) of expiration of the period of validity; b) changes of last or first name; c) discovery of errors in entries; d) unsuitability for further use.

Article 13. In cases of loss or destruction of the PASPORT, its holder is obliged to report this in writing immediately at the *militsiya* organ in his place of residence or arrival for stay.

Article 14. Issuing, receiving or transfer of the PASPORT as a pawn is forbidden.

Article 15. Citizens arriving for residence from one locality to another for a period of more than three days, those who change living quarters within the confines of one and the same inhabited point, or those who have had PASPORTA renewed or exchanged them, are obliged within 24 hours to give up their PASPORTA...to persons responsible for residence registration, for presentation at *militsiya* organs for registration.

Article 22. Residence registration of persons arriving for permanent residence is not permitted, if in their PASPORTA there is no notation of de-registration from the former place of residence.

Article 25. Persons arriving on duty travel, vacation, for treatment, or to Summer homes in the Summer season, are registered without notation or deregistration in the PASPORT.

Article 37. Citizens of the U.S.S.R. who in accordance with Art. 1 of this *polozheniye* are required to have PASPORTA are subject to penalty in administrative proceedings for living without a PASPORT or with expired PASPORT, and also without residence registration. Citizens who have lost their PASPORTA are subject to this same responsibility.

Article 38. Repeated infraction of the established rules for residence registration of the PASPORT by citizens of the U.S.S.R. incurs criminal responsibility...Continued living without PASPORT by persons who are obliged by law to have them, and who earlier have been subject to administrative investigation for this infraction, incurs criminal responsibility....

From the standpoint of their impact upon human freedom these provisions of the *polozheniye o paspor-takh* (and undoubtedly other Articles whose text is still unknown to us) could rank in importance with our Bill of Rights and the emancipation proclamations in both the United States and the Russian Empire in 1861. Unfortunately, these clauses of the Soviet regulations take their citizens back into a repression hardly equalled by the Tsars, not forward into enlightened humanism and regard for the rights of the individual, as did the American legal milestones.

As mentioned in Chapter One, a substantially new

PASPORT issuance applicable to all citizens has been instituted in the U.S.S.R., beginning about January 1, 1976. It is based on a new legal statute (*polozheniye o pasportnoy sistem* = Law Concerning the Pasport System), affirmed by a decree of the Council of Ministers U.S.S.R. dated August 28, 1974, which replaces the 1953 law. The functions of the new legal basis are described by a Soviet publication as follows:

"This legal document answers the evolved needs for creation of conditions for better accounting of the population of the country, and regulation of its movement, in cities and rural localities; it corresponds to the new tasks of perfecting planning of the national economy; and the use of labor resources. The *polozheniye o pasportnoy sisteme* aids in the further development of democratic [sic] principles in the life of Soviet society, the achieving by citizens of rights guaranteed by the Constitution, and the fulfilling of their obligations. It serves to strengthen socialist law and the legal order."[4]

The same source is very specific as to the area of applicability of the new PASPORT version: "The obligation to have a PASPORT is extended to all citizens of the U.S.S.R. who have attained age 16, regardless of where they live—in a city or a rural locality."[5]

The issuance of the new document was begun first to 16-year olds, to persons newly released from military duty, and to repatriates. Persons holding old type PASPORTA which reached expiration after July 1975 have been allowed to continue living on the old document as if it had been extended, until such time as the new PASPORT can be issued to all.

The new PASPORT differs in external appearance and even in title from the version which has been used with little change since 1932. The full name of the document now is "*PASPORT GRAZHDANINA SOYUZA SOTSIALISTICHESKIKH RESPUBLIKIKH*" ("Identity Document of a Citizen of the Union of Soviet Socialist Republics"). The cover of the new issue is described as "dark red, impressed with the gold seal of the Soviet Union and the word "PASPORT."

The same source indicates that a few interesting changes have been incorporated in the 1976 version, but broadly speaking the document and its functions are essentially the same as the earlier form.

Perhaps the most radical change on the surface is that all persons now receive a PASPORT of unlimited validity (*bessrochnyy*) instead of the five-year, ten-year and unlimited assurance of the past. However, in practice the renewal is retained, since the holder must report to the MVD *militsiya* to have a new bearer's photograph affixed in the document, upon reaching age 25, and again at 45.

Another reported major change is the elimination of the former Entry 8, which cites the documents on the basis of which the PASPORT is issued. We can speculate that this is a time and space saving move made possible by the perfecting of MVD controls in recent years.

The only other reported difference is the omission of "place-of-work" cachets which have been a prominent feature of the "Special Remarks" pages of the PASPORT since 1932. The only justification supplied by Rybal'chenko is that more ad hoc employment papers adequately testify to the individual's relation to useful work.

A most intriguing statement by the same source is that the notation concerning relationship of the holder to military obligation is entered in the new PASPORT *by the military commissariat (VOYENKOMAT)*. In the past this entry (5) was made by the PASPORT desk official of the MVD *militsiya*. This could indicate a strengthening of the position of the military in civil affairs.

Another innovation is the entry of the holder's blood type and Rh factor in the PASPORT by health officials, "with the assent of the citizen."

In addition to the stated form and procedural changes in the PASPORT, considerable refinement in the residence registration system *(propiska)* appears to have been instituted in the new legal basis. Perhaps the most significant item is that there now exists a single, unified registration procedure for all parts of the U.S.S.R., city or rural. From the changes described by Rybal'chenko it can be generalized that residence registration has by no means been relaxed or radically altered. The new regulations may perhaps best be described as the result of a process of refinement of the *propiska* system, drawing on the experience of a half century of control over the individual.

FOOTNOTES

1. Robert Conquest *The Soviet Police System*, Contemporary Soviet Union Studies Series, New York, Praeger, 1968, p. 55.
2. *Bol'shaya Sovetskaya Entsiklopediya* 1st ed., vol. 43, p. 199.
3. See Chapter Six, "ZAGS".
4. Rybal'chenko, R.K., *Pasportnaya sistema v SSSR*, Kiyev, "vishcha shkola," 1977, p. 4.
5. Ibid., p. 12.

3

In Chapter Two we mentioned that several pages of the basic identity document (PASPORT) are used exclusively for recording residence registration. In the Russian-language-only version these are pages seven through thirteen. On these pages are entered cachets and handwritten data which play a critical role in the life of the Soviet citizen, information which on the one hand legitimizes him and enables him to live within the law, but on the other restricts his movements and mode of living to the framework which the establishment feels his position in life should be.

As seen in the preceeding pages, every citizen must present himself, either to the *militsiya* police directly, or through an intermediary such as an apartment housing supervisor (*upravdom*), whenever he carries out or even contemplates one of the following actions: 1) moves from locality to another for more than three days' stay; or 2) changes quarters within the same locality; or 3) gets a new or duplicate PASPORT. Such an appearance must take place within 24 hours of such action.

This compulsory residence registration (*propiska*) is no paper tiger. Its teeth are the several applicable passages of the Criminal Code. We begin to understand just how dictatorial and arbitrary the regime can be when we read the actual wording of some of its provisions in regard to residence in cities like Moscow:

> Persons who are refused residence registration for one reason or another are required to leave the populated point within three days, a fact of which they are notified in writing. After lapse of the specified time they are considered in violation of the PASPORT regulations.[1]

The above crime is punishable under Article 198 of the Code. Similar violations, such as forgetting to register on time, subject the citizen to the provisions of Article 192. If deliberate criminal intent is seen by the authorities, additional punishment may be levied, according to Article 196 if a falsified or improper document is involved, or Article 198 if the person lives in a locality where new, more stringent PASPORT rules apply. Moscow city and oblast' were declared such a locality by a Decree of the Presidium of the Supreme Soviet U.S.S.R., dated 8 March 1963. Since that date the *militsiya* there has been empowered to levy punishment on violators of the PASPORT regulations "...without recourse to other administrative commissions." In other words, a citizen can be put into police confinement, or otherwise punished, at the whim of a single police official, with no court process at all.

Of course there was a particular reason for designating the Moscow area as special PASPORT locality. For a generation Soviet citizens from other parts of the

Union have made resettlement in the capital their life goal, and many have succeeded. This has been true especially of demobilized soldiers who, at the end of their conscription period, have managed to lose themselves in Moscow in great numbers, rather than return to their home areas and a lifetime of dreary provincial labor. Some outsiders have estimated the true population of Moscow to be as high as eleven million, if all the unauthorized residents are counted in. On this point, Robert Conquest cites official Soviet references to the fact that the *militsiya's* new powers under Article 198, even before the decree cited above, have been credited with reducing the swollen population of Moscow appreciably, by 10,000 persons in the first half of 1958 alone.[2]

In the preceding chapter we mentioned the provisions of the *polozheniye o pasportakh* which govern residence registration. Let us look again at Article 22 of that regulation, which states:

> Registration of persons arriving for permanent residence is not permitted, if in their PASPORTA there is no de-registration entry from the former place of residence.

From the control standpoint Article 22 has enormous significance. It can and does represent a basic tool for the repression of individual freedom. This restriction on one's choice of residence, taken together with a parallel prohibition on hiring which we shall investigate in a subsequent section, effectively keeps the citizen in his status quo in society.

In actual practice these requirements can give rise to impossibly contradictory situations. For example, an enterprise may offer a good job to a worker from a plant in some other locality. But when its personnel office tries to hire the man it runs into two problems. For one thing this step is impossible if the worker's former employing organ declines to release him and so affirm in the man's Work Booklet and PASPORT. Indeed, such hiring is punishable under provisions of the Labor Code (*kodeks zakonov o trude*). Even worse, the prospective new employee may not be registered for residence, even if the new employer guarantees him company housing. Without a release from the old employer the *militsiya* or housing directorate officials in that locality may well refuse to de-register the individual. Denial of release and de-registration may no longer be strictly legal under present laws, but managements which experience a shortage in labor force may not hesitate to bend the rules in order to hang onto desirable personnel. A screening of the Soviet press often turns up conflicts of this sort. As we shall note in another section the deciding voice in such disputes will be the Party, acting through the local *profsoyuz* (labor union) organization.

Another feature of *propiska* registration in actual practice which seems to have escaped the attention of outsiders, and indeed is scarcely mentioned if at all in the published regulation on PASPORT registration, is temporary *propiska*. This is a practice which seems to have originated in the 1950s, probably first in Moscow and other large urban areas. Under this system new arrivals in such areas receive *propiska* cachets in the PASPORT valid only for short, specified periods, with the terminal date written. The length of temporary registration seems to fit no firm schedule, some lasting less than three months, while other stamps indicate validity for a year or more. The practice is now so customary and widespread that most *propiska* cachets issued in cities contain the words "*propisan vremmeno*" (registered temporarily), or "*propisan postoyanno*" (registered permanently), in their printed texts.

Some of the features of residence registration described here can be seen in our sample PASPORT, of which pages seven through ten contain *propiska* cachets. (See Figure 4.)

The first stamp indicates that the bearer was registered for permanent residence in the housing of a construction directorate in Irkutsk oblast'. A sharp-eyed observer will note here an apparent violation of regulations, which clearly state that residence registration must be carried out upon issuance of a new PASPORT. The issue date of this document is 13 July 1956, some six months prior to the date of the first *propiska* stamp, on 14 January 1957. Carelessness or ignorance on the part of local *militsiya* personnel are possibilities.

The bearer was de-registered *(vypisan)* from the above residence on 15 May 1957, when he obviously left Siberia. On 26 July we see him registered again, but only on a temporary basis, for about 2½ months, by the 18th *militsiya* section in the city of Moscow. Prior to the expiration of this permission he was re-registered by the same organ, this time temporarily for one year, and subsequently for another.

The next two cachets are ordinary *propiska* stamps, without the "temporary" text. They show the bearer changing rooms at the same address. Finally, on December 29, 1962, we find he has de-registered there, and from the final entry was registered without time limit in the 96th *militsiya* section of the city on Leninskiy prospekt, on 15 March 1963. We can only speculate where or how he lived between these last two dates without registration.

From the above actual case history we can see that the bearer was even denied permanent residence status in Moscow for more than 24 months, even though he was registered as employed in a Moscow enterprise for about half of that time. But if his move from Irkutsk to Moscow had come after the Decree of 8 March 1963, our man probably would have been denied temporary residence, and shipped back out to Siberia.

Residence registration is the catalyst which makes the whole concept of the PASPORT system work in real life. This repressive device places the burden of control on the citizen himself, simply by threatening grave penalties for his failure to perform the compulsory registration procedures. It forces him to come to the officialdom, rather than the reverse. And that officialdom is the *militsiya,* a component of the State police armed with extraordinary powers.

A listing of the *militsiya's* powers should particularly concern those Americans who see organs like our F.B.I. and Internal Revenue Service as threats to individual freedom. Conquest has summed up the *militsiya's* functions in the following list:

a) administering the PASPORT system
b) supervision of exilees and those returned from exile
c) law enforcement, with right of arrest, entry and search
d) enforcement of laws on guns, printing devices, seals and stamps, photography, radioactive substances . . .

e) control of all address and information bureaus
f) collaboration with the *upravdomy* (house managers) and *domoupravleniye* (housing directorate), *druzhinniki* (the militia auxiliary, similar to the Chinese "Red Guards"). (And, though not listed by Conquest, with ZAGS, the vital statistics organ.)
g) maintenance of order in public places
h) street traffic control
i) investigation of crime and its prevention
j) tracing lost persons and draft evaders
k) juvenile delinquency, waifs, strays
l) issuance of external travel passports to Soviet citizens going abroad; registration through its visa sections (OVIR) of foreigners in the U.S.S.R. (except for foreign diplomats)
m) detection and expulsion of "anti-social and parasitic elements."[3]

The *militsiya* is empowered to carry weapons and to use them. Also, although seldom seen even by Soviet citizens, there are special *militsiya* troops, armed and quartered in various locations around the country, available for dealing with any eventualities which might threaten the social order.

If any doubts the real might of the *militsiya*, a look at pertinent provisions of the Criminal Code should be convincing. For example, resistance to a member of the *militsiya* (or even to one of the (*druzhinniki*) is punishable, under Article 191/1, by one to five years imprisonment. An attempt on the life of such personnel may incur the supreme penalty (death by shooting), as called for in Article 191/2. Even an insult or an affront to a *militsiya* man is punishable by six months imprisonment (Article 192/1).

As indicated in the above material from Conquest, one of the most potent weapons in the *militsiya's* arsenal of controls is its network of informants. These include the allegedly volunteer militia auxiliaries *(druzhinniki)*, who are in reality organized and directed by the Party at all levels; the housing commandments *(upravdomy)*, who report all activities of the residents in their jurisdiction directly to the *militsiya;* and the "secret collaborators" *(seksoty)* who lurk in all areas of Soviet life—a sort of domestic spy network targeted against the Soviet citizen by his own government. Interested readers can find fuller treatment of this subject in the cited work by Conquest.

The *propiska* system which we have just examined, whereby every Soviet citizen must be registered by the police for place of residence, does not rely only on the use of stamps in the citizen's PASPORT to insure this registration. The other side of the registration coin is the use of "house books," "arrival slips" and "departure slips," and certification of housing managers that housing space actually is available for such registration.

The key device in this scheme is the "house book" *(DOMOVAYA KNIGA)*, which was instituted at least as early as 1940. The encyclopedia definition of the PASPORT which we cited in Chapter One states clearly that residence registration is carried out by inscribing individual citizens in this book. Except for this mention we know little of the legal basis for the house book; presumably its exact description and rules for use are contained in articles of the *polozheniye o pasportakh*

which are not available in normal publication channels. Some informants who have lived under the PAS-
PORT system have shown knowledge of this control
device, but no known exemplar has been seen in the
West, in original or photo copy. From the detailed de-
scriptions and prescriptions for use of other official Soviet records we can assume that it is in the form of an
album or ledger, with each page sewn in, numbered
consecutively, and sealed. The *Great Soviet Encyclopedia* contains only the following brief treatment of the
DOMOVAYA KNIGA:

> ...a book of registration of inhabitants living in a
> house; it is maintained by every city housing au-
> thority which has lodgings. The legal form for resi-
> dence registration and de-registration of inhabi-
> tants is defined by the *polozheniye o paspor-
> takh*...and subsequent statutes...; breaking the
> regulations incurs administrative punishment,
> and in the event of repeated infraction, criminal
> responsibility according to Article 192-A, Part 1,
> Criminal Code of the U.S.S.R.

Keeping the House Book is one of the main tasks of
the *upravdom* of a city apartment building. This official, who on the surface appears to be merely the Soviet counterpart of the concierge or Hausmeister of
Western Europe, is in reality an adjunct of the *militsiya*
as we mentioned above, although nominally an employee of the housing directorate.

From the pertinent regulations, and from the testimony of persons who have lived under the system, we
can reconstruct the procedure which is followed when
a Soviet citizen seeks a place to live in a city apartment

building. He must first report to the *upravdom* and present his PASPORT showing a de-registration cachet from his last residence, and other documentary proof that he is eligible for the desired residence. The *upravdom* then fills out a so-called "arrival certificate" *(listok pribytiya)* and a paper affirming that housing exists in the apartment for the newcomer. This official then takes the last two documents and the PASPORT to the police precinct *(otdeleniye militsii)* for registration at the PASPORT desk. If no problems arise, the PASPORT desk official enters a *propiska* cachet in the proper page of the individual's PASPORT, which is then returned to the bearer by the *upravdom*.

In smaller towns, and where single family housing exists, there may be no *upravdom* as such. But a House Book still is required, even though it must be maintained by an individual house "owner," and any instance of stay by persons other than the family registered there, even for a single night, must be entered in the book. Such books, like those kept by city *upravdomy*, are subject to periodic examination by the housing directorate and the *militsiya*. Whether or not arrival certificates and the corresponding departure affirmation *(listok ubytiya)* must also be filed by heads of households is unclear. Indeed, only a few exemplars of such documents have been seen in the West.

The House Book is obviously an effective and restrictive control device, perhaps the most penetrating invasion of privacy which the Soviet citizen must endure. In a sense *it brings the police scrutiny of the militsiya PASPORT desk right into his home.*

In this and the preceeding section we have had a look inside the Soviet internal identity document system and identified the key devices and procedures which

make it work. Perhaps the best summary is provided by
the following words from Conquest:

> Among these obliged to collaborate with the Militia in running the passport system are: 'house administrators,' the commandants of houses and hostels, administrators of hotels, sanatoria, rest homes, hospitals, children's and invalids' homes, officials of village Soviets, and house owners...
>
> "The internal passport system restricts freedom of movement within the U.S.S.R., serves as an adjunct to the State direction of rural and urban labour, provides a brief case-history of the entire urban population, and can readily be turned against categories of the population deemed undesirable at any given moment.[4]

In succeeding sections we shall consider other areas of life, controlled by documentation and registration procedures which come under the jurisdiction of Soviet organs other than the *militsiya*. Nevertheless, in almost all these aspects of human regimentation we shall see the iron presence of the *militsiya*, peering into every move which the Soviet citizen makes in the course of his life.

FOOTNOTES

1. Ugolovnyy kodeks RSFSR. Ofitsial'nyy tekst...Moscow, 1966, Explanation 7 to Article 198, p. 423.
2. Robert Conquest, *The Soviet Police System*, New York, Praeger, 1968, p. 65.
3. Ibid., p. 31 ff.
4. Ibid, p. 57 ff.

4

In the preceding pages we have considered the PAS-PORT system which prevails in the U.S.S.R., with its corollary devices—the residence registration procedures known as *propiska,* and the seldom-mentioned "house book" *(DOMOVAYA KNIGA).* The control which these institutions give the government over the everyday life and movements of all Soviet citizens should be self-evident; however, we should not make the mistake of thinking that this regimentation exists for regimentation's sake alone, that the Communist Party is interested simply in knowing where everyone is out of mere curiosity or suspicion. There is another motive for the iron discipline of the PASPORT system, an obvious one when we consider Marxist-Leninist principles. As we mentioned when discussing the Russian concept of individuality, a "person" is defined as a sensible being, able to speak, *and having the capacity to work.* The very core of Communist philosophy treats of the useful work which each citizen performs for the State. It follows that the dictatorship of the proletariat must know where every citizen is, and that he is available for useful work. This is perhaps the main raison d'etre of the PASPORT system.

But Marxism-Leninism requires that the State's control and supervision over working life extend far beyond the mere "locator service" which the PASPORT system affords. The Party must also be able to place and utilize every individual in a work situation it deems most advantageous to the socialist society as a whole. And it must be certain that once so placed the worker will be kept on in that capacity as long as needed, not allowed to drift about at his own whim. Otherwise the entire structure of Soviet state planning on which the Communist economy rests would be built on sand.

In this section we shall look at the system of laws and control devices which the Soviet regime has developed to insure the reliability of the labor force. It represents the genius of Lenin and his associates in constructing the original framework of proletarian control, refined since then during a half-century of Party experience in regimenting the Russian worker. Briefly stated, we shall be examining key passages of the Labor Code and other laws relating to adherence to work regulations, and the personal documentation employed to assure such compliance. Beyond this we shall have a look at the very heart of the Communist labor edifice—the *profsoyuz.*

Soviet labor law makes much of the Communist system's claimed solicitude for the worker, especially its ability to free him forever from the fear of unemployment and the uncertainties of the free-market economy with its periodic crises. It is not our purpose here to debate such claims or to produce countering propaganda. We are concerned rather with the other side of the coin—namely what the Soviet worker gives up in personal freedom and human values by being included in the Communist system of "guaranteed labor." Let us look at some of the legal provisions of that system.

Section *(glava)* 2 of the Labor Code *(KODEKS ZAKONOV O TRUDE)* states the Soviet case as follows:

> The right of citizens of the U.S.S.R. to work is assured by the socialist organization of the people's economy, by the steadfast growth of the production forces of Soviet society, the removal of the possibility of economic crises, and the liquidation of unemployment.
>
> Workers *(rabochiye)* and employees *(sluzhashchiye)* realize this right by means of concluding a work contract in enterprises, establishments and organizations.

The work contract mentioned above is the legalistic device which the Soviet government employs to assure work continuity, and yet appear to allow the individual some freedom of choice and action. As we shall show, this is indeed little more than appearance; the worker's power to exercise his own judgment and will is very narrowly limited by the details of the work contract, as defined by several articles of the Labor Code, and by the realities of Party control over employment at every level.

In reality the worker is subject to the provisions of two contracts. One, which he is not obliged to sign, is a collective contract *(KOLLEKTIVNYY DOGOVOR)*, an agreement which exists between every Soviet enterprise and the local level of the *profsoyuz* (the so-called "professional union" affiliated with whatever ministry governs the production of the enterprise). Every worker in the enterprise is included in the provisions of the collective contract, whether or not he is a member of the *profsoyuz*. This contract is essentially a Communist Party document which asserts the Party's control over every aspect of the work activity, from pay scales to protective clothing, from production norms to paid vacations. The collective contract is defined in Article 7 of Section II of the Labor Code.

The individual labor contract, the one which is actually signed by the worker, is a more significant item in determining the life-style and career of the individual citizen. The actual wording of Article 8, Section III of the Code speaks for itself. The contract is defined as:

> ...an agreement between the worker and the enterprise, establishment or organization, according to which the worker obligates himself to carry out work in a defined capacity, qualification or specialty, with submission to the internal work arrangements. The enterprise, establishment or organization is obligated to pay the worker a wage and to assure conditions of work envisioned by the labor laws, the 'collective contract,' and the agreement of the parties.
>
> Article 10 cites the legal periods of validity of work contracts: (1) for an indefinite period; (2) for periods not over three years; and (3) for the time required to finish a specific task.

At first glance this legal basis for all labor in the Soviet Union seems like a fairly reasonable proposition, a quid pro quo situation with no real threat to individual freedom. But upon closer examination small doubts begin to creep in. What happens when a worker wishes to leave his job for personal reasons? If his contract is for an indefinite period is he not then bound by law to work at the given enterprise in perpetuity, as a paid but none the less indentured servant of the State? And how about the worker with a contract of specified time length? May he leave before the end of the period, and what is his freedom of choice in finding new employment at the end of that time?

We find some enlightenment in Article 15 of the Code, entitled "Bases for Curtailment of the Work Contract," which lists seven possible bases for breaking the individual work contract (*TRUDOVOY DOGOVOR*):

1) agreement of the parties
2) expiration of the period of work time cited in points 2 and 3 of Article 10
3) call-up of the worker for military service
4) breaking of the contract under provisions of Article 16
5) transfer of the worker to work of a different nature
6) refusal by the worker to move to another locality
7) judgment of a court, sentencing the worker to deprivation of freedom or corrective labor at some location elsewhere.

If we analyze these justifications, against a background of experience with persons who have lived under the system, we can exclude most of them as offering any protection to the worker's personal freedom. Points 1, 5 and 6 offer him no guarantee of release at his own initiative, and are really bases which allow the administration of enterprises to discharge unwanted workers without incurring the opposition of the all-powerful *profsoyuz* organs. Points 3 and 7 promise the worker only a more repressive future. Point 2 seems to allow choice to those finishing a work contract of specified duration, but nowhere is there any indication of either rights or compulsions in resuming his work career. Point 4 calls our attention to Article 16 of the Code.

Article 16 is entitled "Breaking of the Work Contract by Initiative of the Worker or Employee." One of its two provisions states that contracts concluded for definite periods may be broken by the worker only in case of illness or incapacity, or if the administration violates the labor regulations, or ". . . for other important reasons." But again there is silence as to his reemployment.

The other provision of this Article states:

> Workers and employees have the right to break the work contract concluded for an indefinite period, after having given the administration of the enterprise written notice two weeks prior.

If the wording of Article 16 can be taken at face value it does indeed appear that the great majority of Soviet workers, those who work under contracts of indefinite validity, have the right to quit any job, after giving two weeks notice. However, this does not jibe with the reported experience of most former Soviet citizens. Most found it difficult to be released for personal reasons. It is true that some Work Booklets have been seen with the entry "released according to personal wish" (*uvolen po sobstvennomu zhelaniyu*), citing Article 44 of the Code as it was applied in the forties and fifties. But these cases generally involved family hardship, movement of a spouse to another area, etc. There is little doubt that in most other situations the employing organization could find ways to bar release at the worker's own initiative. And, as Robert Conquest points out, absenteeism and willful departure from work constitute criminal offenses prior to April 1956.[1]

What is the real situation since 1956? As Western observers have noted, the Soviet regime has been continually concerned with the problem of keeping the work force stable under the regulations adopted in 1956. Turnover and fluidity of personnel have been consistently high, especially in some areas. One consequence of this trend may be the curiously contradictory wording of a recent re-working of the labor regulations, entitled "Model Regulations of Internal Labor Order for Workers and Employees of Enterprises, Establishments and Organizations" (Decree of the Council of Ministers, State Committee for Questions of Labor and Wages, 29 September 1972, No. 258).

This updated official attitude to the Soviet worker and his right to quit work is worth citing in spite of its apparently conflicting statements. Article 9 repeats the traditional language of earlier versions:

> Workers and employees have the right to break the work contract after having notified the administration of this in writing two weeks prior. At the end of this period they may properly cease work, and the administration...is required to issue the worker his Work Booklet.

However, the same article contains the following new statement in its heading [italics supplied by author]:

> *Curtailment of the contract may take place only for reasons provided for in the legal system.*

Further, Article of the same section states:

> In the U.S.S.R. freedom of choice in type of work
> and profession is assured, *taking into account the
> interests of society.*

The stressed sentences in these Articles appear to be
an attempt to reimpose a curb on quitting at the
worker's own volition, while at the same time retaining
the earlier idealistic wording concerning the worker's
right to leave upon two weeks' notice. The vagueness
and potential for wide interpretation which the language of these Articles contains suggests that some
fundamental swing back to the strict control over
work-force mobility which existed before 1956 may be
in progress.

Another hint of a stiffening of official policy in regard to labor freedom may be embodied in an *(UKAZ)*
(decree) of the Supreme Soviet of the R.S.F.S.R. dated
15 March 1972, entitled "Proceedings on Placing into
Effect the Labor Code of the RFSFR." Article 4 of this
decree reads:

> Upon curtailing of the Work Contract after intro-
> duction of the Labor Code of the RSFSR, the bases
> for curtailing the Work Contract are decreed in ac-
> cordance with Articles 23, 29, 31, 32, 37, and 254
> of the Code. Other supplementary bases for the
> curtailing of the Work Contract are decreed in ac-
> cordance with legal actions of the USSR and the
> RFSFR by which such bases are established.

From the very appearance of this language it seems
some tightening of labor mobility is underway.

The totality of Soviet labor law, from which we have extracted a few citations to illustrate a viewpoint, is referred to as *"ZAKONODATEL'STVO SOYUZA SSSR I SOYUZNYKH RESPUBLIKH O TRUDE"* (Labor Legislation of the USSR and the Union Republics). This collection constitutes an enormous mass of regulations, decrees, clarifications and interpretations designed to insure the maximum utilization of the labor force. But still another level of work regulations exists, a body of labor dogma which bears particularly on the individual in every phase of his working life, in many respects to a greater degree than do the provisions of the Labor Code. This is the quasi-legal collection of continuing regulations which emanate from the "All-Union Central Union of Professional Unions" (VTsSPS), an organ directly subordinate to the Central Committee of the Communist Party, *not to any ministry.* We shall take a look at this organization and its effect on the mobility of the individual in a subsequent section.

For the worker, one of the most tangible and constant reminders of the power and presence of the legal codes is the Work Booklet which has been referred to in passages quoted above. We may gain some idea of the importance which the regime attaches to this control device when we see some of the many pages of regulations and instructions which pertain to this personal document, especially the penalties connected with its misuse. After a detailed look at the booklet itself, we shall return to the official prescriptions concerning its use.

The Work Booklet *(TRUDOVAYA KNIZHKA)* is a document approximately 8.8 × 12.5 centimeters, although over the years the dimensions have varied somewhat in different editions. The cover also, once a simple cotton fabric, now is a textured plastic material. Its color however has remained a shade of gray ever since the inception of the document in 1939. The paper which makes up the pages is cheap unwatermarked stock, and the printing is quite ordinary. The booklet is bound together by wire staples (three in our exemplar). At the top left of the outside cover appears the great seal of the U.S.S.R., and below it to the right the title TRUDO-VAYA KNIZHKA. In our sample (Figure 6) the title is repeated in the Uzbek language (MEKHNAT DAFTARCHASI), since the place of issue was in the Uzbek S.S.R.

Page One calls for the full name of the bearer, in the regular PASPORT order *(familiya, imya, otchestvo)*. Next come the year of birth, then the bearer's education and profession. In the illustrated Work Booklet (Figure 7) the instruction "underline" for the education entry has been ignored and the entry "6 classes" written instead. This is because the bearer completed more than four years of the beginning school, but less than the eight to ten of the usual middle school. Our bearer's occupation is given as "carpenter."

The remaining entries on the first page call for the bearer's signature and the complete date of fill-out of the booklet. We shall comment on this and other dates in this document when we compare it with the regulations governing issuance.

The next eight pages are headed "*svedeniya o rabote*" (work data); they contain a complete summation of the bearer's labor history. This data is arranged under four columnar headings: 1) entry number, in order; 2) year, month and day; 3) "data concerning hiring, transfer and release (with indication of reasons)"; 4) documentary basis for the entry, and its number.

Figure 6

Трудовая книжка
Фамилия
Имя
Отчество
Год рождения
Образование: начальное, среднее, высшее
(подчеркнуть)
Профессия
Подпись владельца Трудовой книжки
Дата заполнения Трудовой книжки

Figure 7

Our Work Booklet begins this section with a statement concerning the bearer's prior work record: "Work experience comprised 7 years before entrance into Construction Directorate No. 18"

The documentary basis for this entry is given simply as: "from (the bearer's) words." (See Figure 8.)

The next two entries (numbered 1 and 2) are by the Construction Directorate No. 18, Mirzachul' *sovkhoz* construction combine; they read as follows:

1. 1957 VIII 26 Enrolled as carpenter, 6th category; Order No. 219 of 26 VIII 57; senior inspector of the personnel." This official, Datsenko, signed the entry.

2. 1959 V 9 Released due to family circumstances; Order no. 181/8 of 9 V 59; official of the personnel section." Signature of this person, Abubakirov.

Comments on the dates of these entries will be in order when we compare them to the regulations.

Pages ten through thirteen of the booklet are entitled "Information concerning incentives and awards." The layout of these pages is similar to that on the pages of employment data, with four columnar headings. In the illustrated booklet (Figure 9) we see four entries made by the same Construction Directorate No. 18:

1. 1957 XII 30 gratitude proclaimed for overfulfillment of social obligations

2. 1958 II 23 gratitude proclaimed for non-loss of work and active participation in social work

3. 1958 VI 7 awarded a money prize in the sum of 175 rubles for overfulfillment of the plan and ahead-of-plan roofing of a building ["roofing"—the handwritten Russian is unclear]

4. 1959 IV 17 awarded a money prize in the sum of 150 rubles for overfulfillment of the plan and good work.

| № записи | Дата | | | Сведения о приеме на работе и увольнении | работу, перемещениях по (с указанием причин) | На основании чего внесена запись (документ, его дата и номер) |
	Год	Месяц	Число			
1	2				3	4
				До поступления в СМУ № 18 общий трудовой стаж составляет 7 лет		со слов
1.	1957	VIII	26	СМУ № 18: Зачислен 6-го разряда Ст. инспектор	Мирзагульсовхозстрой изолировщиком Ок! Д---	пр. № 219 от 26/VIII-57. (Доценко)
2.	1959	V	9	Уволен обстоятельствам Нач. Ок!	по семейным ей вопросам.	пр. № 181/8 от 9/V-59. (Абубакиров)

Figure 8

In a Russian-language-only Work Booklet there remain just three more pages, those which contain the full text of the Decree *(POSTANOVLENIYE)* of the Council of People's Commissariats which put the Work Booklet system into effect on December 20, 1938. However, in our example sixteen more pages follow, representing in the Uzbek language an exact duplication of all the Russian pages we have examined.

The Decree of 1938 is of such fundamental importance to the Soviet worker that a translation of its chief provisions is in order:

1. From 15 January 1939 on Work Booklets are to be introduced for workers and employees of all State and cooperative enterprises and establishments, to be issued by the administrations of the enterprises.
2. Into the Work Booklets are to be entered the following information concerning the holder of the Work Booklet: family name, first name, patronymic, age, education, profession, and data concerning his work, his transfer from one enterprise to another, the reasons for such transfer, and also concerning incentives and awards received by him...
4. Work Booklets are prepared in a single model for the entire U.S.S.R. The text of the Work Booklets is printed in Russian and in the language of the given Union or Autonomous Republic.
5. Fill-in of Work Booklets is done in that language in which the business of the given enterprise is carried on. In the event business is conducted in the language of a Union or Autonomous Republic, the Work Booklet is simultaneously filled in in Russian.
6. ...The administration may hire workers and em-

№ записи	Дата			Поощрения и	награждения	На основании чего внесена запись (документ, его дата и номер)
	Год	Месяц	Число			
1		2			3	4
				СМУ № 18 гре	с̄о. Мирзочулмеевкозенрой-	
1.	1957	XII	30	За перевыпол	нение соц. обяза-	пу № 401
				тельный обе	звяка благодар-	от 30/XII 57 г.
				ность		
				Жаг. ок!	*[подпись]*	/ Абубакиров /
2.	1958	II	23	За безупречну	ю работу и	пу № 69
				активное уса	сти в обществе-	от 23/II 58
				ной работе	объявлена	
				благодарность		
				Жаг. ок!	*[подпись]*	/ Абубакиров /
3.	1958	VI	7	За перевыпол	нение плана и	пу № 240
				досрочный ввод	жилья пу	от 7/VI 58 г.
				мировал де	нежной премией	
				с сумме 175	рублей *[подпись]*	/ Абубакиров /
				Жаг. ок!		

Figure 9

СВЕДЕНИЯ О ПООЩРЕНИЯХ   И НАГРАЖДЕНИЯХ

№ записи	Дата			Поощрения и	награждения	На основании чего внесена запись (документ, его дата и номер)
	Год	Месяц	Число			
1	2				3	4
4	1959	IV	17	За перевыпол- чв. и короссу- рован денежи- в сумме 150 №02 ох!	нение плана и работу преми- ной премией рублей. *(подпись)* /Трубанова/	ц № 158 от 17/IV.-59г.

Figure 9 continued

ployees only upon presentation of a Work Booklet. Persons entering work for the first time are required to present to the administration a certificate *(SPRAVKA)* from the housing directorate or village council concerning their last occupation.

7. ...For persons entering work for the first time in the future, the Work Booklet must be issued not later than five days after hiring.

8. Work Booklets are maintained for all workers and employees who work more than five days in an enterprise, including seasonal and temporary workers...

9. The Work Booklet is kept in the administration of the enterprise and upon release of the worker or employee is issued to him personally.

10. Work Booklets are filled out by the administration of enterprises and establishments in accordance with the following regulations:

    a) Year of birth, middle and higher education are shown only on the basis of documents. Elementary education may be indicated from the bearer's own words.

    b) In the column 'profession' is shown the basic occupation in accordance with the worker's own deposition.

    c) In the section 'Information concerning work' is entered first of all the following notation under Heading 3: 'General work experience upon hiring, prior to hiring in the enterprise which issues the Work Booklet, comprises so many years.' In Heading 4 is written accordingly 'Confirmed by documents, so many years experience, and from the worker's own words, so many years.'

d) Further there is entered, in the form of a heading, the designation of the enterprise issuing the Work Booklet. Under this heading are entered notations on the date of hiring in the given enterprise and on job transfers which took place before fill-out of the Work Booklet. Notations in the section 'Information concerning work' are formulated after the following model: in Heading 2 is indicated the date of hiring, transfer or release; in Heading 3 is written 'Taken in such-and-such shop (division) in such-and-such capacity', or 'transferred to such-and-such shop (division) in such-and-such capacity', or 'released for such-and-such reason'; the reason for release must be indicated in exact accordance with the formularizations of the Labor Code or in the form of a reference to an Article (Point) of that Code; in Heading 4 is indicated the order concerning hiring, transfer or release.

All notations made after issuance of the Work Booklet must be made by the administration soon after publishing of the order. Notations in succeeding places of work are formulated in exactly the same manner.

g) All notations in the Work Booklet are done in ink.

11. After issue of the Work Booklet, payment in the amount of 50 kopecks is collected from the holder by the administration.

12. In case of loss of the Work Booklet as a result of careless keeping, the holder of the Booklet is subject by the administration to administrative punishment, such as a fine in the amount of 25 rubles.

A person who has lost his Work Booklet is re-

quired to report this without delay to the administration (at the place of work). Not later than 15 days after this reporting the administration issues a new Work Booklet with the inscription 'Duplicate'.
13. All sums, arising either from the collection of payment for issue of the Work Booklet or from collection of fines for loss of Work Booklets, go to the State income.
14. Illegal use of Work Booklets, their transfer to other persons, their forgery or falsification—are punishable in criminal procedure.
15. Organizations and enterprises receive the Work Booklets from the corresponding commissariats [ministries today]. (See Figure 10.)

In the generation which has passed since the *TRUDOVAYA KNIZHKA* was introduced, this device has evidently proved its effectiveness as a control over the working force, as evidenced by the relatively few changes which have been made, either in the document itself or in the procedures governing its use. Indeed, from the standpoint of the printed text of the booklet, there has been no change at all. However, experience with its use has led to some enlargement and amplification of the rules laid down originally in the *postanovleniye* of 20 December 1938, most of which we have just cited. The latest re-working of these regulations is contained in an "Instruction Concerning the Format of Keeping Work Booklets in Enterprises, Establishments and Organizations." This edict is based on several decrees of the State Committee of the Council of Ministers on Questions of Labor and Wages (Numbers 620 of 9 July 1958; 232 of 20 May 1961; 20 of

2 February 1963; 185 of 2 July 1963; 132 of 23 March 1966), and a joint decree with the All-Union Central Union of Professional Unions of 15 January 1970. Some of the more interesting additions and extensions of the original rules are the following from this Instruction:

1. ...Work Booklets are kept also for non-State employees, in cases where they are subject to social insurance.

2. The Work Booklet is the basic document which characterizes [testifies to] the work activity of the worker or employee.

3. ...In the event there is discovered a notation in the Work Booklet concerning the last places of work which does not correspond to the present Instructions, the holder of the Work Booklet must apply to the administration of the enterprise at the former place of work, with a request to correct the inaccurate or inexact notation. The administration of the new place of work is required to supply him necessary help.

   ...persons released from the Soviet Army are required to present to the administration their Military Service book (*VOYENNYY BILET*).

The Instruction then gives three pages of detailed guidance in filling out the Work Booklet. From these we cite only the following significant extract governing fill-out upon release of a worker:

6. A notation concerning release of a worker is made in accordance with the following rules:

   In Heading 1 is placed the number (in succession) of the notation.

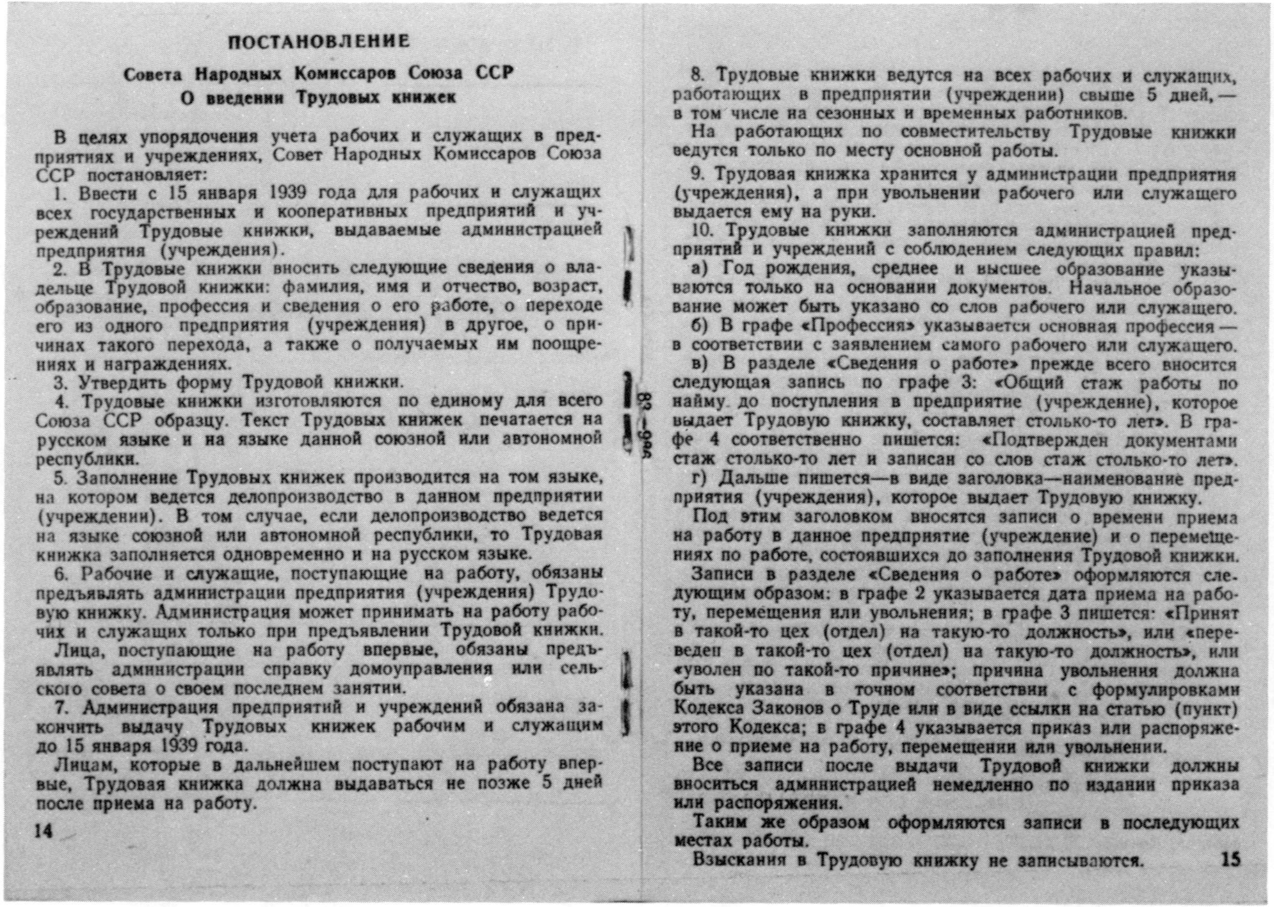

ПОСТАНОВЛЕНИЕ

Совета Народных Комиссаров Союза ССР
О введении Трудовых книжек

В целях упорядочения учета рабочих и служащих в предприятиях и учреждениях, Совет Народных Комиссаров Союза ССР постановляет:

1. Ввести с 15 января 1939 года для рабочих и служащих всех государственных и кооперативных предприятий и учреждений Трудовые книжки, выдаваемые администрацией предприятия (учреждения).

2. В Трудовые книжки вносить следующие сведения о владельце Трудовой книжки: фамилия, имя и отчество, возраст, образование, профессия и сведения о его работе, о переходе его из одного предприятия (учреждения) в другое, о причинах такого перехода, а также о получаемых им поощрениях и награждениях.

3. Утвердить форму Трудовой книжки.

4. Трудовые книжки изготовляются по единому для всего Союза ССР образцу. Текст Трудовых книжек печатается на русском языке и на языке данной союзной или автономной республики.

5. Заполнение Трудовых книжек производится на том языке, на котором ведется делопроизводство в данном предприятии (учреждении). В том случае, если делопроизводство ведется на языке союзной или автономной республики, то Трудовая книжка заполняется одновременно и на русском языке.

6. Рабочие и служащие, поступающие на работу, обязаны предъявлять администрации предприятия (учреждения) Трудовую книжку. Администрация может принимать на работу рабочих и служащих только при предъявлении Трудовой книжки.

Лица, поступающие на работу впервые, обязаны предъявлять администрации справку домоуправления или сельского совета о своем последнем занятии.

7. Администрация предприятий и учреждений обязана закончить выдачу Трудовых книжек рабочим и служащим до 15 января 1939 года.

Лицам, которые в дальнейшем поступают на работу впервые, Трудовая книжка должна выдаваться не позже 5 дней после приема на работу.

14

8. Трудовые книжки ведутся на всех рабочих и служащих, работающих в предприятии (учреждении) свыше 5 дней, — в том числе на сезонных и временных работников.

На работающих по совместительству Трудовые книжки ведутся только по месту основной работы.

9. Трудовая книжка хранится у администрации предприятия (учреждения), а при увольнении рабочего или служащего выдается ему на руки.

10. Трудовые книжки заполняются администрацией предприятий и учреждений с соблюдением следующих правил:

а) Год рождения, среднее и высшее образование указываются только на основании документов. Начальное образование может быть указано со слов рабочего или служащего.

б) В графе «Профессия» указывается основная профессия — в соответствии с заявлением самого рабочего или служащего.

в) В разделе «Сведения о работе» прежде всего вносится следующая запись по графе 3: «Общий стаж работы по найму, до поступления в предприятие (учреждение), которое выдает Трудовую книжку, составляет столько-то лет». В графе 4 соответственно пишется: «Подтвержден документами стаж столько-то лет и записан со слов стаж столько-то лет».

г) Дальше пишется — в виде заголовка — наименование предприятия (учреждения), которое выдает Трудовую книжку.

Под этим заголовком вносятся записи о времени приема на работу в данное предприятие (учреждение) и о перемещениях по работе, состоявшихся до заполнения Трудовой книжки.

Записи в разделе «Сведения о работе» оформляются следующим образом: в графе 2 указывается дата приема на работу, перемещения или увольнения; в графе 3 пишется: «Принят в такой-то цех (отдел) на такую-то должность», или «переведен в такой-то цех (отдел) на такую-то должность», или «уволен по такой-то причине»; причина увольнения должна быть указана в точном соответствии с формулировками Кодекса Законов о Труде или в виде ссылки на статью (пункт) этого Кодекса; в графе 4 указывается приказ или распоряжение о приеме на работу, перемещении или увольнении.

Все записи после выдачи Трудовой книжки должны вноситься администрацией немедленно по издании приказа или распоряжения.

Таким же образом оформляются записи в последующих местах работы.

Взыскания в Трудовую книжку не записываются.

15

Figure 10

д) Поощрения и награждения записываются за время со дня поступления в предприятие (учреждение), которое выдает Трудовую книжку. При этом записываются только единовременные индивидуальные поощрения и награждения, связанные с работой в предприятии (учрежденин). Премии, предусмотренные системой заработной платы, не записываются.

е) При увольнении все сведения о работе, о поощрениях и награждениях, внесенные за время работы в предприятии (учреждении), заверяются подписью его руководителя (или специально уполномоченного им лица) и печатью предприятия (учреждения).

ж) Все записи в Трудовой книжке производятся чернилами.

11. За выдачу Трудовых книжек взимается администрацией предприятия (учреждения) с владельцев книжек плата в размере 50 копеек.

12. В случае утери Трудовой книжки в результате небрежного ее хранения владелец Трудовой книжки подвергается администрацией предприятия (учреждения) в административном порядке штрафу в размере 25 рублей.

Потерявший Трудовую книжку обязан немедленно заявить об этом администрации (по месту последней работы). Не позже 15 дней после заявления администрация выдает новую Трудовую книжку с надписью: «Дубликат».

13. Все суммы, поступающие как от взимания платы за выдачу Трудовых книжек, так и от взимания штрафов за утерю Трудовых книжек, поступают в доход государства.

14. Незаконное пользование Трудовыми книжками, передача их другим лицам, подделка и подчистка их — караются в уголовном порядке.

15. Трудовые книжки предприятия и учреждения получают от соответствующих наркоматов и учреждений.

16. Постановление Совета Народных Комиссаров Союза ССР от 21 сентября 1926 года «О трудовых списках» (Собр. Зак. СССР 1926 г. № 66, ст. 502; 1929 г. № 35, ст. 315)—отменяется.

Председатель СНК Союза ССР В. МОЛОТОВ.

Управляющий Делами
СНК Союза ССР И. БОЛЬШАКОВ.

Москва, Кремль. 20 декабря 1938 года.

83—986

МЕХНАТ ДАФТАРЧАСИ

Фамилияси ....

Исми ....

Отасининг исми ....

Туғилган йили ....

Малумоти: бошланғич, ўрта, юқори
(тагига чизилсин)

Касби ....

Меҳнат дафтарчаси эгасининг имзоси

....

Меҳнат дафтарчаси тўлғазилган вақт

«..........» .... 19..........й.

Figure 10 continued

In Heading 2 is presented the date of release. Month and day of release are noted only by Arabic, two-digit numbers. E.g., for a worker released in the year 1965, in the month of May, on the eighth day: in Heading 2 is noted "1965, 05, 08." Another case might be thus: "1965. 12. 18."

In Heading 3 is shown the reason for release. Notations in Work Booklets concerning the reasons for release must be done either in exact correspondence with the formularizations of existing legislation, or in the form of a reference to the corresponding Article or Point of the law. (At this point in the Instruction a footnote appears, amplifying the previous statement: "In accordance with Article 39 of the Labor Code concerning reasons for release, entry in the Work Booklet must be shown not only in exact correspondence with the formularizations of the legislation in force, but also by reference to the corresponding Article and Point of Law)".

These last specifications would seem to bear out the belief that release of a worker for personal reasons is coming under increasingly close scrutiny by the regime.

Section II of the above Instruction covers an area which apparently had not been envisioned in the original decree. It deals with the "Insert" (*VKLADYSH*), which consists of an added page or pages of printed text for use in the event the sections for "Information concerning work," or "Information concerning incentives and awards" become completely filled in. The following Article spells out the procedure:

20. The Insert is sewn into the Work Booklet, and filled out and kept by the administration of the

enterprise...at the place of work of the worker or employee, in the exact manner as with the Work Booklet. Concerning every Insert sewn into a Work Booklet there is placed a stamp at the top of the first page of the Work Booklet, measuring 10 × 25 centimeters, with the inscription 'Insert Issued.' For each succeeding issuance of an Insert a second, and a third stamp is entered, etc.

The writer has seen exemplars of the "Insert" issued as early as the 1940s.

We can perhaps summarize the chief restrictions on the working life of the average Soviet citizen upon which we have touched in this chapter, as follows:

Choice of occupation: Theoretically this is left to the desires of the individual, but subject to the operative phrase: "taking into account the interests of society." This wording is open to an almost infinite number of interpretations.

In applying for a job: It is impossible to be hired without showing either a proper Work Booklet or, for young people, a *spravka* from the housing directorate or village council. Further, the person must produce his PASPORT for entering of a hiring cachet (which may not be entered unless the PASPORT contains a stamp showing release from a previous place of employment).

In applying for release: Although theoretically this is left to the wishes of the individual, in practice release is possible now only "...for reasons provided for in legislation." Also, the latest Instruction calls for tighter control over the permissible reasons for release.

Loss of the Work Booklet: The burden of proof and correction of faulty entries is on the bearer by law, regardless of who made the erroneous notation.

It is difficult to assess the actual practice of Soviet enterprises against the legal backdrop we have outlined. Interrogations of defectors and other former Soviet citizens rarely ever went into such detail in covering an individual's background, even in Western intelligence services. Generalizations are especially difficult; some particularly resourceful individuals have been known to be able to circumvent most controls over work mobility, while others found themselves bound indefinitely to a given job. Other factors have also created problems to the regime in completely instituting the provisions of the labor codes in all areas, for example, differences in living modes in non-European regions, geographic conditions, etc.

If we analyze the few entries in our sample of the Work Booklet we can see some indication of a lag of practice behind law in a non-Russian area (in this case the Uzbek S.S.R.).

Our exemplar seems to have been done correctly by the local personnel section, with the entries all in ink and in the proper headings. But the very first page shows one outstanding departure from the regulations. The date of fill-in is stated as being "14 March 1959." But from pages 2 and 3 we see that the bearer was hired as a carpenter 6th category by the issuing organization (SMU Nr. 18) on 26 August 1957. Since Article 7 of the Decree of 20 December 1938 states categorically that a worker must be issued a Work Booklet "not later than 5 days after hiring," this delay of over a year and a half is a clear violation. Nor are we dealing with a replacement booklet issued because of loss or destruction of an original; in that event the first page would be prominently stamped "DUPLICATE," as specified in the Instructions. This discrepancy is probably just an indication of provincial carelessness or procrastination.

The entry concerning release was legal enough at the time the document was issued, but under the new prescriptions of the Instruction on Work Booklets of 1970 this wording would be insufficient; beside the notation "released due to family circumstances" a reference to the pertinent Article of the Labor Code must be added.

Otherwise, our sample *TRUDOVAYA KNIZHKA* seems quite valid, with all the necessary citing of order numbers, attesting signatures of proper officials, and the validating cachets of the enterprise. It is obvious from this exemplar, and from the hundreds of others which have been seen in the West, that the Work Booklet system is in effect everywhere in the U.S.S.R., that there is strict adherence to the regulations which govern it, and that this system is very effective in controlling the mobility of the labor force in the Soviet Union.

Mention should be made of a couple of other documents which figure in the question of work choice and mobility. One of these is the Collective Farm Worker's Labor Booklet *(TRUDOVAYA KNIZHKA KOLKHOZNIKA)*. This document (not shown) is less of a control paper than a record of work performed by the individual, for purposes of pay computation.

This booklet is a set of stapled sheets, without a plastic or cloth cover. Its text gives the name of the bearer and the *kolkhoz* (collective farm) organization to which he belongs. Most of the pages simply contain spaces for recording (by the kolkhoz brigade chief) of the work the bearer has accomplished in a given month, by "work days" *(trudodni)*. Since the average kolkhoznik has not been *pasportized* until now and therefore could not move about freely, he had no need of formal documents showing details of his employment history. The kolkhoznik's Work Booklet would be less than useless to present to a prospective new employer in some other area than the individual's home village.

By contrast, another document used in connection with work status is very strictly controlled. This is the Certificate of Incapacity for Work *(LISTOK NETRU-DOSPOSOBNOSTI)*, a paper used to identify persons as physically unfit for work, for periods ranging from three days to several months or longer. The LISTOK performs two functions: it relieves the bearer of the obligation to be engaged in socially useful work, and simultaneously serves as the basis for receiving social security insurance in lieu of wages. The *Great Soviet Encyclopedia*, 1st edition, definition provides some details:

> The *listok netrudosposobnosti* (also known familiarly as *bol'nichnyy listok* and *byulleten'*) is the sole document which certifies the right of a worker or employee to freedom from work and to assistance, in all cases of temporary incapacity for work. According to Soviet legislation concerning State social insurance, release from work with rights to assistance is extended: for illness, for accident (industrial or in everyday life); for leaving because of a sick family member; and for quarantine; for sanatorium treatment; for pregnancy and childbirth.
>
> Medical organizations are forbidden to issue any other kinds of certificates in place of the *listok*. The *listok* is issued by physicians of medical organizations of the Ministry of Health and the Ministry of Transport. Issue of the *listok* by paid polyclinics and hospitals is forbidden...
>
> Each *listok* has a serial [letter] and number. It consists of a bound portion *(koreshok)*, which is re-

tained by the medical enterprise, and a tear-off portion which is issued to the patient.

Individual physicians have the right to issue the *listok* for a period of no more than 3 days each time, and all together for no more than 10 days for a given case of illness. Extension of the *listok* beyond this period is done by a consultative commission of physicians...

Profsoyuz organizations check the correctness of issuance of *listki netrudosposobnosti* by medical enterprises.

The very few examples of the LISTOK which have been seen in the West (consisting of the tear-off *talon* only of course) were single sheets of paper with the special watermark used for the PASPORT, and underprinted with a fine, pale blue design. As the above encyclopedia definition confirms, these exemplars had a serial consisting of two Cyrillic letters followed by Arabic numbers. On the reverse side at the bottom appear the name of the State printing house "GOZNAK". These details give some indication of the importance which attaches to this seemingly routine medical document. We must remember that this is the sole legal proof of a special status in the Soviet Union, that is, that a citizen of working age is freed from the obligation to be engaged in useful work (and of course entitled to financial support while not working). Of key importance is the fact that final control over the use of this release document is vested, not in the Ministry of Health, but in the *profsoyuz* system, as evidenced by the final sentence of the definition quoted above. In the next section we shall have a close look at the *profsoyuz* as a major instrument of control over the individual.

There are several other personal documents in use in the labor field, to attest to various aspects of workers' activities. One of these is the *KOMANDIROVOCH-NOYE UDOSTOVERENIYE* (or *komandirovka* in everyday parlance), which is an official duty travel paper issued by State enterprises to certify that one of their employees is moving from one point to another on work assignment. The *komandirovka* may be either a printed or typewritten document, depending on the size of the establishment. Its text states that so-and-so is travelling to a given place on business, with the exact dates specified, and sometimes the nature of the assignment. Without such a paper, or another we shall name below, a Soviet citizen travelling any great distance from his home area can expect to be questioned by *militsiya* or other officials as to the justification for moving about. Document checks are routine on all long-distance transport—rail, air or water.

The other document which can support an individual's presence away from home is the *OTPUSKNOY BI-LET* (leave ticket). This is a single-sheet item similar to the *komandirovka*, either printed or typed, and issued by the personnel office of the enterprise which employs the worker. The text states that the holder is presently in regularly scheduled vacation leave (*ocherednyy otpusk*) from such date to such date. Depending on the circumstances, the document may also specify a vacation resort (*kurort*) to which the bearer is to travel. In the section on the *profsoyuzy* we shall see how such desirable escapes from the tedium of Soviet working life are assigned to selected lucky workers.

One last labor document should be mentioned. This is the *KHARAKTERISTIKA*, which is defined as "an official document containing an evaluation or conclusion about a person's work or social activity." It is issued by an employing organization to a (usually former) employee, to attest to his performance of work, in the manner of a letter of recommendation in the West. The *KHARAKTERISTIKA* usually gives a more detailed and readable description of the person's activities than does the Work Booklet. It is usually typewritten on the organization's letterhead like the above travel documents, and signed and sealed with the cachet of the organization.

In these times it is pertinent to mention that all the labor controls mentioned in this chapter apply with equal force to women. The Soviet system does not envision that the typical female should stay home during her useful life, but rather that she work alongside males except for those times when she can be excused for childbirth and temporary care of newborn infants. As Conquest has noted, by 1964 women had come to constitute 49% of the working force in the U.S.S.R.[2] Thus, a probable majority of able-bodied Soviet women share the dubious privileges of the Labor Contract and of carrying a TRUDOVAYA KNIZHHA.

FOOTNOTES

1. *Industrial Workers in the U. S. S. R.*, Robert Conquest, New York, Praeger, 1967, p. 107
2. Ibid, p. 134

5

The *Kodeks Zakonov o Trude* and the many other regulations, instructions, decrees and explanations which collectively make up the body of Soviet labor law provide the regime with very broad powers over the individual worker, as we have shown in the previous section. But some may ask, what authority makes use of these powers to regiment and utilize the vast Soviet working mass? Is it the managements of the individual enterprises, the plant administrations, who oversee the compliance of all parties to the demands of this stern network of laws?

The answer of course is that it certainly is not the managers of industry who interpret and enforce the labor laws; indeed, some of those regulations contain provision to punish industry officials for infractions of the codes. The real authority in all matters of working life, and the production of goods, is the *profsoyuz*, at whatever level such questions may arise. The *profsoyuz* organization, from top to bottom, has final say in this area, regardless of which ministries and their subordinate industries may be involved.

The next question for many will then be: what is the *profsoyuz*? A realistic, accurate definition of this institution is not easy to find. In Soviet official jargon the *profsoyuz* is a "professional union." But it would be a mistake to equate this term with our concept of a labor union, whose function is to work for higher worker pay and improvement of working conditions, etc., without direct concern for the problems and wishes of management—production quotas and profits. The Soviet *profsoyuz* on the contrary is concerned primarily with fulfillment of production norms and adherence to the canons of the Communist work ethic. The *Great Soviet Encyclopedia*, 1st edition, (vol. 35, p. 162) says simply:

> Professional unions in the U.S.S.R. carry out all their work under the leadership of the Communist Party of the U.S.S.R., which organizes and directs the forces of Soviet society.

What this means in practical terms is that, although every factory, shop, enterprise, *sovkhoz* and *kolkhoz* in the country is subordinate to a particular ministry, the *profsoyuz* council in residence in that enterprise is working for other masters, *namely for the Central Committee of the Communist Party of the Soviet Union*. The *profsoyuz* is, so to speak, the blue-collar arm of the Party. Its representatives at the lowest working level (the so-called *pervichnyye organy profsoyuza*) are in some ways similar to shop stewards in a closed shop in American industry, but with incomparably greater powers. A recent *profsoyuz* publication gives the number of its councils at this level in the U.S.S.R. as 587,000. Included in this number are 33,000 *profsoyuz* councils formed in recent years on collective and State farms.

Lenin, who is credited with originating the idea of the *profsoyuz*, saw its function as follows:

> It is an educational organization, an organization of involvement, of training; it is a school, a school of directing, a school of management, a school of Communism.

Among its powers the *profsoyuz* has the sole authority to plan, implement and regulate worker pay, work safety, workers' insurance and compensation, plant dining rooms, housing, recreation and physical culture. (Most Americans are probably not aware that this last area is under the jurisdiction of "professional unions." This includes complete control of all sports activities at all levels—especially the far-flung empire of competitive sports programs which grooms the "Masters of Soviet Sport" and aims at domination by these Soviet athletes in the Summer and Winter Olympic Games and other international competitions.)

The Party periodically reaffirms the significance it attaches to the *profsoyuz* structure. Thus, in its XXIVth Congress in April 1971, the KPSS stated:

> Noting the great significance of the *profsoyuz* as the most massive organization of workers, the Congress views it as necessary to improve its activities once again.
>
> The Party will further concern itself that the *profsoyuzy* successfully fulfill their role—as a school...of Communism. The *profsoyuzy* are called upon to strengthen work in the further development of the country's economy, actively to at-

tract workers to the direction of industry and social work, to improve the organization of Socialist competition, to teach the Communist relationship to work. . . .

The parent *profsoyuz* body, the Central Union of *Profsoyuzy* (VTsSPS), sees the following areas of activity as its responsibility:

1) the building of Communism
2) establishing the material base of Communism
3) improving labor conditions and the material well-being of workers
4) educating the workers in Communism
5) the struggle for an international *profsoyuz* movement

The *profsoyuz* at the plant or farm level is the workhorse of Communism; its activists are the people who translate Party resolutions into human action. They constitute a vast bureaucracy, unceasingly busy in every field of Soviet endeavor, doing no tangible, productive work themselves, but constantly prodding others to do so. They are the real power in all industrial-labor relations, able to dictate absolutely to management and labor alike. When Five Year Plans, annual production quotas, and ad hoc resolutions to boost output come down from the Party and via the various ministries, *profsoyuz* council members organize all manner of programs and slogans to goad the working masses into increased action. "Improve Socialist competition!" is a key theme of the *profsoyuz*, which has made use of devices such as the Stakhanovite system of rewarding output beyond the norms, and the more recent and more typically Communist concept of the "*Subbotniki*". An official definition of the activity of the latter reads: "The voluntary, collective unpaid fulfilling of some sort of socially useful work (originally carried out on Saturdays)". The term derives of course from the Russian word for Saturday, *Subbota.*

Westerners may wonder how the *profsoyuz* is able to work its will on the vast army of workers, seemingly by little more than the endless repetition of corny slogans. In reality its effectiveness comes from a shrewd application of the "carrot-and-stick" principle, balancing the offering of rewards and incentives with tough threats for failure to conform and produce. Under Soviet conditions these two motivations indeed become inextricably merged. A worker is well aware that by producing beyond the required minimum norms, and by belonging to the local *profsoyuz,* he assures himself of a livable pension in his old age. By the same token, he knows that if he doesn't extend himself to this demanding and distasteful extra effort, upon reaching his retirement he may find that the pension to which he is lawfully entitled may habitually be bogged down in bureaucratic paperwork, or even lost altogether. The *profsoyuz* has a long memory, and it alone administers the pension system.

Beyond these negative powers of the *profsoyuz* there are the compulsions of the Criminal Code. Its articles on the Work Contract which we mentioned in the previous section can be invoked against the occasional stubborn or chronic malingerer. And there are even sterner punishments in the vague passages of the Criminal Code which deal with infractions of Communist labor discipline.

One of the most effective incentives in the arsenal of the *profsoyuz* is its control over annual vacations and vacation travel. The *profsoyuz* council, not the plant management, determines when a worker will take his two weeks vacation, and who will get the prized vacation trip warrants *(putevki)* to resorts at the seaside or in the mountains. *Putevki* are assigned on a centralized basis and issued to the local *profsoyuz* councils quarterly for awarding to the chosen workers. The following extracts from official *profsoyuz* formularizations describe how this is done:

16. . . . Factory, plant and local committees of the profsoyuz pay the entire costs of the putevki once each quarter, upon receipt of the putevki for that quarter.

17. Republic, krai, oblast and city profsoyuz councils send out the putevki to profsoyuz organizations in accordance with the affirmed plan.

    The sending out of putevki is done in such a manner that the factory, plant and local profsoyuzy receive the putevki not later than one month before the beginning of their validity.

18. The sending of the proforganization is done by registered mail with a fee of 10 kopecks for each putevka. Putevki may be issued by profsoyuz representatives with a warrant signed by the president and the senior bookkeeper of the profsoyuz council and fastened with a seal. . .

19. Upon sending of the putevki or their issue by warrant, . . . an invoice is made out in two copies. In the invoice is shown the name of the sanatorium, pension, rest home or polyclinic, and the numbers of the putevki, their quantity, and the value and costs of each. The invoice is sent by mail separately from the registered packet with the putevki. . .

21. Upon receipt of the putevki by mail from the profsoyuz council which directs resorts, . . . the proforganization is required to send it a written
message confirming receipt of the putevki, not
later than the day following receipt.
22. Resale or assignment or putevki to other organizations is forbidden. . .
22-a. Sanatorium chiefs see to it that the "return *talon*
portions of the putevki" are issued to vacationers
and patients, showing the actual time of stay in the
resort or rest home, and in cases of early
departure—the reasons.

This power over every aspect of vacation and recu-
perative travel is perhaps the chief reason why many
Soviet workers bother to become members of the local
profsoyuzy, with the consequent requirement to pay
dues and to take part in all kinds of political-action ses-
sions. Even the dullest of Soviet laborers can figure out
where his interests lie when he learns how the issuance
of the coveted vacation travel *putevki* is determined. In
every shop, priority in issuance is given to the following categories of workers:

> . . . members of profsoyuzy, working disabled vet-
> erans of World War II, innovators and 'leading
> workers' of industry, personnel people, industrial
> engineering-technical workers, working persons
> disabled on the job, and those who systematically
> donate blood.

Practically speaking then, for the mass of Soviet
workers, this amounts to one of two avenues of ap-
proach to a decent vacation once a year: either by giv-

ing a great deal of one's blood literally during the year, or figuratively by enduring the dreary concomitants of membership in the *profsoyuz.*

This membership is shown tangibly by the issuance of a dues booklet (PROFSOYUZNYY BILET), a facsimile of which is shown in Figures 11 through 15. Our exemplar is a two-language version issued in the Uzbek S.S.R. We shall examine this document, after first citing the definition of it given in the *Great Soviet Encyclopedia,* 1st edition (vol. 35, pp. 171–2):

A document certifying the membership of the bearer in a professional union. The profsoyuznyy bilet contains basic information about the member of a profsoyuz, his work status, notes concerning his being taken on or off the rolls of a (profsoyuz) organization. *P. bilety* for all profsoyuzy of the U.S.S.R. are printed according to a single model, both for Russian and the national languages, among those the languages of the Autonomous Soviet Republics. A unique numeration of *p.b.'s* is carried out in each profsoyuz. Upon transfer from one profsoyuz to another, the *p.b.* is not exchanged, and does not lose its validity.

Most exemplars of the PROFSOYUZNYY BILET seen over the years have had maroon woven-cloth covers. As seen from Figure 11, the cover text contains the Communist slogan "Proletarians of all lands, unite!" at the top, in Russian, then beneath this the same in the republic language. Below this in larger letters is the document's title, also in both languages. At the bottom are the initials "VTsSPS", standing for "All-Union Central Union of Professional Unions".

ПРОЛЕТАРИИ ВСЕХ СТРАН, СОЕДИНЯЙТЕСЬ
БУТУН ДУНЁ ПРОЛЕТАРЛАРИ, БИРЛАШИНГИЗ
ПРОФСОЮЗНЫЙ БИЛЕТ
КАСАБА СОЮЗ БИЛЕТИ
ВЦСПС

Figure 11

Figure 12 shows the first two pages, the second being an Uzbek-language equivalent of the first. At the top are the seal of the organization with the bust of Lenin, the words "*professional'nyye soyuzy SSSR*" and the title of the document.

The first three lines call for the name of the *profsoyuz*. Our sample contains a stamped entry here: "Of the workers of the food industry." Below this are two lines for the bearer's last name and patronymic. Next is a line for "profession", which lists our bearer as "carpenter." Below is entered the year of his entrance into the *profsoyuz*, in his case 1952. Following this are lines for the name of the organ which issued the document. The entry here reads: "F.Z.K. Bakery NO. 1". The *bilet* was issued 20 January 1960. Besides the signatures of the president of the *profsoyuz* committee and of the bearer, there appears a round validating cachet of the chief (*zavkom*) of the committee.

The next nine pages of the document contain spaces for affixing of the monthly dues stamps. Our example shows that its bearer paid about 100 rubles in dues in 1960 (including the stamps for November and December, which are missing and the spaces marked "stamps lost"). (See Figure 13.)

Since the bearer of this booklet first became a *profsoyuz* member in 1952, this is apparently his second *bilet*. This is likely because there is space for only nine years' in each booklet.

The twelfth and thirteenth pages of this exemplar are reserved for "notations concerning enrollment and removal from the rolls." Page twelve shows our man taken on the rolls at the "*khlebzavod (bakery) Nr. 1)*" on 12 June 1967.

ПРОФЕССИОНАЛЬНЫЕ
СОЮЗЫ СССР
ПРОФСОЮЗНЫЙ БИЛЕТ
№ 51169
Профсоюз Рабочих пищевой промышленности
Фамилия
И., О.
Год рождения
Профессия
Год вступления в союз
Наименование организации, выдавшей билет
Председатель комитета
Личная подпись
СССР КАСАБА СОЮЗЛАРИ
КАСАБА СОЮЗ БИЛЕТИ
Фамилияси
Исми ва отасининг исми
Тугилган йили
Касби
Союзга кирган йили
Билетни берган ташкилот
Комитет раиси
П. у.

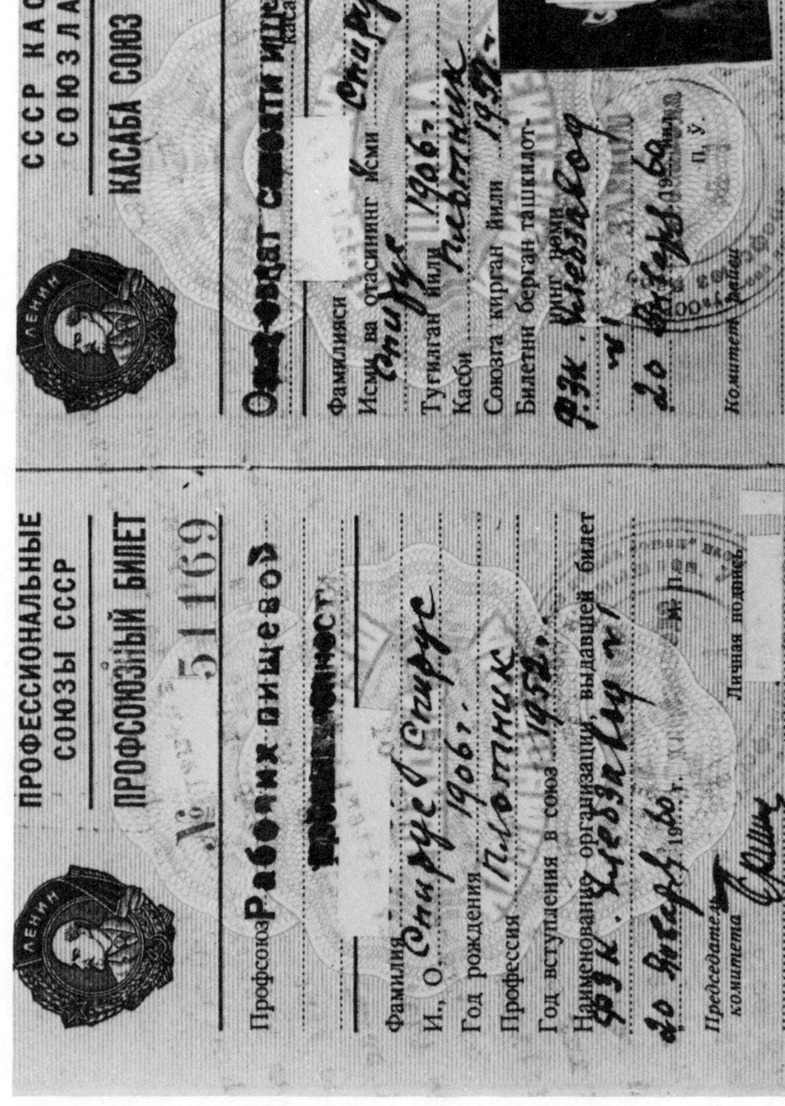

Figure 12

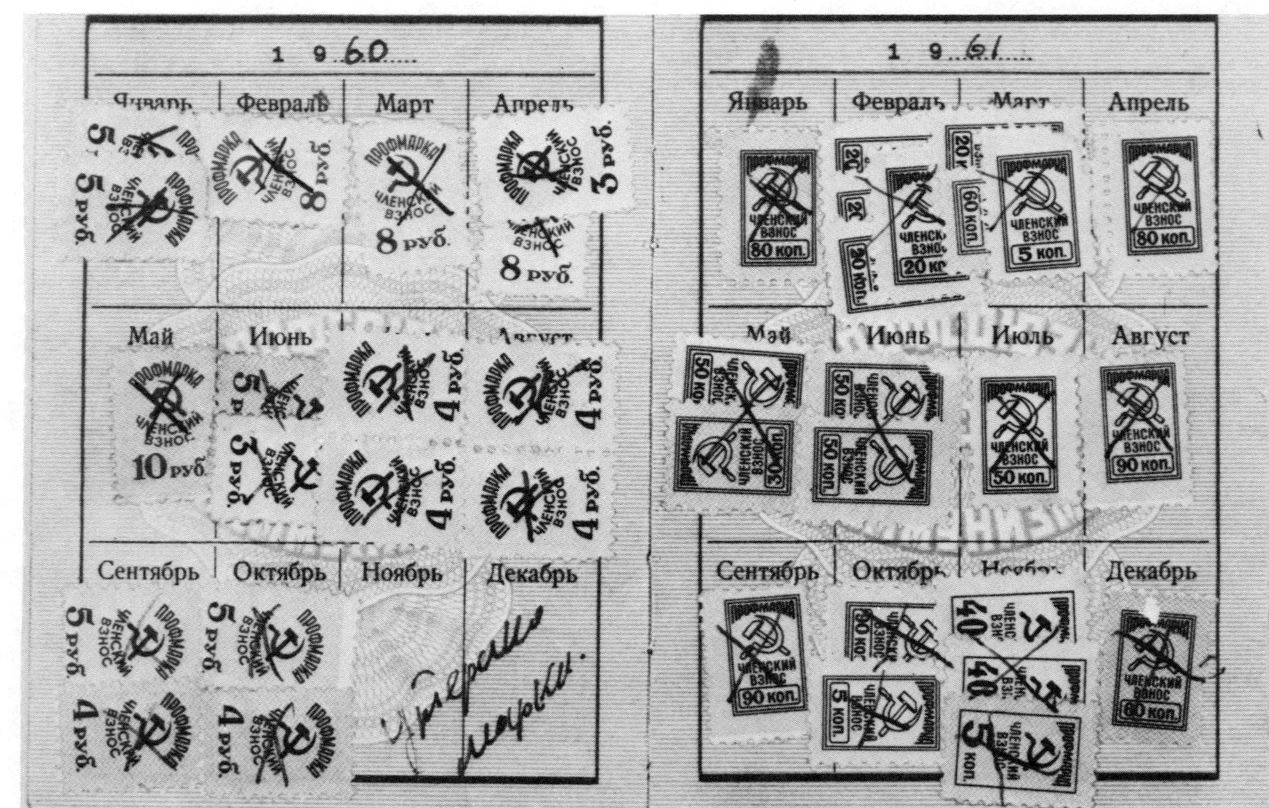

Figure 13

1 9...........			
Январь	Февраль	Март	Апрель
Май	Июнь	Июль	Август
Сентябрь	Октябрь	Ноябрь	Декабрь

УЧЁТГА ҚАБУЛ ҚИЛИШ ВА УЧЁТДАН ЧИҚАРИШ ҲАҚИДА БЕЛГИЛАР
ОТМЕТКИ О ПРИЕМЕ НА УЧЕТ И СНЯТИИ С УЧЕТА

Дата	Учётга қабул қилган ва учётдан чиқарган касаба союз ташкилотининг номи. Наименование профорганизации, принявшей на учет и снявшей с учета	Имзо, печать, Подпись, печать
	12 v-57г. принят на учет Кузаев!	

Figure 14

Figure 15

The final page of the document (see Figure 15) is headed "notes". Our exemplar contains none. At the bottom of the page is printed the fact that, like all *profsoyuz* booklets, it was produced by the State Printing House "GOZNAK", in 1959, in an Uzbek edition.

Readers will undoubtedly have noticed that every page of the booklet has a colored underprinting which proclaims the official motto of the *profsoyuz*: "Profsoyuzy—the School of Communism".

An accounting by the Statistics Sector, Organizational-Instructional Division of the VTsSPS in 1972 shows that as of 1 January 1972, a total of 98,022,100 Soviet workers were carrying this booklet. The carrot-and-stick principle works very well indeed.

6

It would seem from the material introduced in the preceding chapters that the Soviet citizen is more than adequately scrutinized and controlled by the documents and procedures we have discussed, without any further activity on the part of the State. However, the fact of the matter is that we have treated only some of the more important personal documents and the controls systems which lie behind them. But, for the sake of conciseness, only two more types of documents will be examined, in this section and in the following chapter on draft status documentation.

In treating the PASPORT we saw that in most cases the basis for issuance of a Soviet citizen's first PASPORT, at age sixteen, is a birth certificate. It follows then that the organization which is charged with the keeping of birth records is an important link in the chain of control over the movements of citizens. This is true of course to varying degree of the vital statistics registry of any civilized nation, but in the USSR, with its obsessive pre-occupation with the identity and whereabouts of the individual, archive-keeping of birth, marriage, divorce and death data takes on an added dimension.

The centralized vital-statistics organization in the Soviet Union is invariably referred to as "ZAGS", an acronym from *"zapis' aktov grazhdanskogo sostoyaniya"*, which we may translate approximately as "registry of civil-condition documents". The term antedates Communist rule by generations. Once again, perhaps the best definition of ZAGS is that given in the relevant entry in the *Great Soviet Encyclopedia*, 1st ed. (vol. 2, p. 4):

> The registry, by special State organs, of birth, death, marriage and divorce, and other data. In Russia obligatory registration of data bearing on civil condition was introduced in 1722. Up to the time of the Great October Socialist Revolution it was in the hands of Church organs (of various persuasions). Only under Soviet rule, when separation of church from state was introduced, was the registry of the most important data relating to civil condition transferred to State organs. In 1918 the first Codex of laws concerning civil status, on marriage, family and guardianship, was issued. Since 1926 decrees concerning civil condition documents constitute a section of the republic codes of laws on marriage, the family and guardianship. Registrations of births, deaths, marriages, divorces and adoption in cities and raion centers are carried out by city and raion divisions of ZAGS, and in villages and workers' settlements by village councils. The Ministry of Internal Affairs' (MVD) Division of Registry of Civil Condition Documents manage the works of all these ZAGS organs...

The most recent body of law on vital statistics registry is the *Kodeks zakonov o brake, sem'ye i opeke RSFSR* (Legal Code on Marriage, Family and Guardianship, RSFSR) referred to above, plus Articles from the Civil Code, and decrees and Instructions issued on the subject since 1946. Among the more significant provisions of the Codex are the following articles:

113. The entry books for civil condition documents are kept in two copies...

117. The keeping of the books for civil condition documents is controlled by an Instruction issued by the (Ministry) of Internal Affairs, in agreement with the Ministry of Justice.

117-a. Responsible officials are subject to criminal responsibility according to Art. 111 of the Criminal Code for groundless failure to record a civil condition of birth or death, and for non-presentation within the established time—or presentation of incorrect—data concerning the actual movement of population.

Responsibility for assuring the timely and correct registration of births and deaths (informing the population as to periods and protocol of registration, indicating cases of evasion of registration, the correct conduct of official records, etc.), is entrusted, in cities to the chief of the city or raion office of ZAGS personally, and in rural localities, to the secretary of the corresponding village or settlement council personally.

Since 1958 the primary responsibility for control of the ZAGS apparatus at the top has been in the hands of the Ministry of Justice, but there is no reason to believe that the MVD's partnership in ZAGS activity is at all weakened, or that any ZAGS files at any level are not immediately accessible to the MVD or any other police organ. Strictly speaking, there is no Union-wide legal basis for the conduct of ZAGS work; just as with the Labor Codes which rest upon the model of the *Kodeks zakonov a trude RSFSR*, there is only a Code Concerning Marriage, Family and Guardianship of the RSFSR. ZAGS officials in the other constituent republics apparently just follow the prescriptions of the RSFSR laws.

A *postanovleniye* No. 524 of the RSFSR Council of Ministers dated 7 June 1957 decreed that the several Councils of Ministers of the autonomous republics in the RSFSR, and the oblast, krai and city executive councils, assure the preparation and supply of file documents on vital statistics, blank certificates of birth, death, marriage, name change, etc. It charged these organs and their subordinate ZAGS offices with "registration of documents of strict accountability (certificates of birth, marriage, death)," and entrusted the leadership to the Division of ZAGS in the RSFSR Ministry of Justice (*Otdel po ZAGSam Ministerstva Yustitsii*). Presumably a comparable hierarchy exists in each of the constituent republics.

An earlier decree, dated 8 January 1946, gives the following specifications for the actual certificates issued by ZAGS: "Blanks (of the birth certificates) are printed on State-seal paper (*na gerbovoy bumagi*) in Russian, and also in the language of the corresponding autonomous republic."

We are fortunate in having access to the basic document which governs the keeping of ZAGS archives and the issuance of certificates, regulations which literally describe the procedures down to the last comma. This

116

special legal document, entitled *Instruktsiya o po-
ryadke registratsii aktov grazhdanskogo sostoyaniya*
(Instruction Concerning Registration of Vital Statistics
Records), appears to consist of 131 Articles.[1] From
some of these Articles, and from certain additional directions contained in the so-called "Methodical Letters
of the Ministry of Justice" *(Metodicheskiye pis'ma
Ministerstva yustitsii RSFSR)*, issued in 1958 and 1959,
we gain an insight into the shadowy archival world of
ZAGS and the procedures its personnel follow in insuring that the whereabouts of every Soviet person is cata-
loged from the moment he draws breath at birth until
somebody declares him no longer useful to the State,
namely dead.

Legal responsibility for reporting vital statistics
events to the proper ZAGS office is placed ultimately
on the ordinary citizen, as usual, with secondary responsibility charged to others such as relatives, housing managers, neighbors and physicians. The penalties
for failure to observe the rules are alluded to in Article
7 from the General Section of the Instruction:

> 7. Upon reporting of cases of evasion of registration
> of birth or death, and also non-observance of the
> periods for registration...established by law,
> without significant reasons, a protocol is formu-
> lated, which is sent to the Executive Committee of
> the respective Council of Workers' Deputies, for
> decision as to the levying of punishment.

Details of the actual fill-in of vital statistics ledgers
are laid out in Section VIII of the Instruction, entitled
"Regulations for Fill-in of Vital Statistics Blanks."
Some of these should be cited for a better understanding of Soviet bureaucratic philosophy as regards
record-keeping on human beings:

78. Blank pages for vital statistics entries are prepared according to forms appended to this Instruction, and bound in separate ledger books. The quantity of pages is shown at the end of each volume. The books are sewn together and sealed with the wax seal of the Executive Committee of the city or raion Council of Workers' Deputies.

79. Blanks of the vital statistics records consist of first and second (tear-off) exemplars, each of which is numbered with one and the same number in order upon registration of the legal document. The numeration of vital statistics entries is begun with the first number, and continues in order in the course of the year from 1 January until 31 December, inclusively.

   For each type of registration a separate numeration is kept.

80. Upon spoilage of a blank vital statistics record the succeeding blank is filled out. Spoiled blanks (both copies) are left in the ledger . . .

81. . . . All heading(s) of the blanks are filled out with exhaustive answers. Omissions or abbreviations of separate words, also erasures, are forbidden. Headings in which negative answers to questions are given are filled out with the word "no" (*nyet*).

82. Last name, first name and patronymic are shown in full, and are based on presented documents. Rendering first name and patronymic in abbreviated form is not permitted.

83. (ethnic) nationality is shown according to the PASPORT. In the absence of a PASPORT, nationality is shown according to the nationality of the parents.

These directions are still only general ones. For entry-by-entry instructions the ZAGS employees on the working level are guided by the separate rules with illustrations for issuing each type of document. For example, in Section III of the Instruction are shown facsimiles of both the pages in the ledger for birth recording, and of the birth certificates themselves.

Section IV gives the same examples for marriage entries and certificates; Section V does likewise for adoption; Section VI for divorce; and Section VII delineates the all-important procedures for registration of death and issuance of the death certificate.

At this point some may ask why we make such an issue of the manner in which vital statistics records are kept in the Soviet Union. After all, birth, marriage, divorce, adoption and death records are maintained faithfully here in the United States, and few people probably feel any sense of repressive control over the individual by the government.

The answer to this lies in centralism. In the United States and most other free-world countries, birth, marriage and death records are the sole responsibility of town, city or county officials. Even the individual States ordinarily exercise no oversight over such records, assuming the local officials observe the pertinent state statutes in carrying on their work. Normally vital statistics records are not duplicated at higher governmental levels (although in some areas original documents may be microfilmed and the film stored elsewhere as a safeguard in case of destruction of the original records by fire). Requests for extracts of local entries on the part of Federal or State bodies, or even by individuals, are honored, usually for a fee. But broadly speaking there is no centralized vital statistics system in this country under which every last birth and death in every nook and corner of the country is routinely extracted and sent to higher jurisdictions for central control of the population. If a man dies in Florida, an official death entry is made in the locality where he died, but no copy is sent to the little town in Ohio or Montana or Maine where he was born, and above all *none is sent to a central archive in Washington*.

Quite the opposite is true in the Soviet Union. It is not an exaggeration to state that the local ZAGS offices exist primarily to record and pass on to higher echelons the raw data on human condition generated in their towns and villages. This is readily evident from Section XI of the ZAGS Instruction, which is entitled "Responsibility for Registration of Vital Statistics Documents and the Accounting for Blank Certificates":

105. Not later than the second day of each month, village (and settlement) councils of workers' deputies send to the raion or city ZAGS offices the second copies of birth, marriage, adoption and divorce, and also second copies of registrations of death with the physicians' certificates of death and with accompanying reports. In the report is show the quantity and number of registrations sent by the council.

    If no vital statistics registration of any kind was made in the territory of the village council in the reporting month, a line is drawn through the report.

106. On the basis of the second copies of vital statistics registrations presented by the village councils, and of registrations produced by the ZAGS Division, a report is created each month on Form 97, in three copies, concerning the total of registrations of vital

statistics. In the report is shown the numbers and quantity of all registrations of birth, death, marriage and divorce,for the Divisions (or office) of ZAGS, and for each village council separately, including the returned and corrected ones. The report is signed by the chief of the ZAGS division.

The second copies of the birth, marriage, divorce and death registrations (with the physicians' certifications of death), together with the first copy of the Form 97, are delivered not later than the seventh day of the month to the Council of Ministers of the Autonomous Republics, krai executives councils...for checking their correctness by ZAGS inspectors, and for transfer to the corresponding statistical directorate. The copy of the report Form 97 is sent to the raion inspector of TsSU (Central Statistical Directorate).

Simultaneously, the second copies of the vital statistics registrations of adoptions and of first and last name change, are sent to the Councils of Ministers of the Autonomous Republics..., and after checking are transferred to the ZAGS archives of the Autonomous Republic...

As outlined in the above Articles, every change in human condition, from birth through death, in every city and hamlet of the RSFSR (and by analogy throughout the USSR), is reviewed in detail at the highest levels of government, that is, by the Councils of Ministers of the Autonomous Republics or the executive councils of the regions and oblasti, within thirty seven days of occurrence at the maximum. *This centralization of information on the personal lives of all Soviet citizens makes complete the State's control over them.* The ZAGS archival network, operating in conjunction with the PAS-

PORT and residence registration systems of the *militsiya*, and the employment regimentation afforded by the Work Booklet and the Labor Contract, effectively fills in any control gaps which might arise from changes in individual citizens' civil status.

The Central Statistical Directorate mentioned in the Instruction provides the State with further data on the individual through the All-Union Census. The first such census in modern times was that begun in 1959, when a vital need existed to locate and identify many thousands of citizens who had been displaced from their home areas by World War II and the chaotic state of Soviet society in the postwar years. Since the 1959 census and subsequent nose-countings the regime is finally in a position to properly utilize the resources given it by the PASPORT, labor registration, and ZAGS archival systems, to fit together the raw data from them into a complete mosaic of control.

Naturally such a capability involves a massive bureaucratic establishment. Treatment of this subject is beyond the scope of this paper of course. However, an article which appeared in the newspaper *Pravda* in 1976 may be apropos. It described a planned new building to be erected in Smolensk, an eleven-story affair to house the archives for Smolensk oblast. The account did not specify which governmental organs would share the space, but it is a safe bet ZAGS will be among them.

Where and how ZAGS stores its material is described in Section XII of the Instruction already cited, entitled "ZAGS Archives". Some of the pertinent articles are:

114. Vital statistics records (document ledgers) are
     preserved:

a) first copies—in the archives of the raion and city divisions (*otdel* or *byuro*) of ZAGS;

b) second copies—in the ZAGS archives of the Autonomous Republics, regions and oblasti.

115. In the archive of a ZAGS otdel or byuro are kept books with the first copies of registry documents compiled by the otdel or byuro in the course of the year, plus books which arrive in the otdel or byuro from village and settlement councils...at the end of the year.

In the otdel and byuro ZAGS archives are kept also the ledgers of pre-Revolutionary birth records (*metricheskiye zapisi*).

116. Registry books arriving at the otdel or byuro of ZAGS from village or settlement councils, and registry books of the otdel or byuro, are held on the account of the archives budget and are stored in chronological order separately by type of document, for each village council and raion center.

117. In the ZAGS archive of the Autonomous Republic, region or oblast are kept the second copies of vital statistics records produced in the territory of the given republic, region or oblast, plus the *metricheskiye knigi* (pre-Soviet birth record ledger). Second copies of document records arrive in the archive of the Autonomous Republic, region or oblast ZAGS from the corresponding Statistical Directorate once a year, not later than 1 December for the preceding year in assembled form—by city and village councils for each raion, and also by type of registration and in numerical order.

120. The preservation of registrations (and pre-Revolutionary books) in the archives of ZAGS ot-

dely and byuros and also in the archives of the Autonomous Republics, regions and oblasti, is established as 75 years.

Upon expiration of this period the books are sent to the State Archive.

Given the Soviet obsession with collecting control data on the individual, we can probably assume that all such material sent to the State Archive is preserved there ad infinitum.

Before leaving the subject of ZAGS, it should be mentioned that the facsimiles given in the ZAGS text for the information of employees involved in vital statistics registration may accurately represent the actual pages of the records books, but this is not true of the illustrations of the certificates issued to the citizen. The general layout of text entries is roughly similar, but of the many exemplars of actual certificates of birth, marriage, etc., seen by the writer, none closely resembled the facsimiles given in the cited ZAGS work.

The genuine articles are more elaborately printed, and are underprinted on watermarked stock with the "GOZNAK" imprint. These physical features are considered of critical importance in the ZAGS registration system, as is evident from the following Articles of the Instruction, Section XI:

107. Blank certificates (*svidetel'stva*) are documents of strict accountability; therefore the listing, preservation and distribution of them must be organized in such a manner that any possibility of loss or theft is excluded.

108. Upon receipt of blank certificates by the executive committee of the city of raion council, a commission is set up to check the correspondence of the received blanks with their accompanying doc-

uments. Then a formal paper (*akt*) is drawn up concerning receipt of the blank certificates. In case defective blanks are noted (absence of or damage to the security network—underprinting—, printed text, presence of duplicated numbers, blanks with deformed type, incorrect trimming or format), errors or non-conformity of the serial letters and numbers on the blank to the Goznak label on the packages, an official paper is prepared in two copies. One copy, with the Goznak label and the defective blanks, is sent to the Council of Ministers...

The handling of blank ZAGS certificates at the lowest working level is interesting for its aura of melodrama:

113. Blank certificates are preserved in non-flammable cabinets or iron boxes. In non-working hours the non-flammable cabinets or iron boxes are kept sealed. Only persons responsible for keeping of the blanks have access to them, and in their absence, only the direct superior of the designated person.

In case of loss or theft of blank certificates, notice is sent, on the same day, to the executive committee...which through the *militsiya* organs takes measures for investigation of the lost or stolen certificates, and informs the Council of Ministers...of what has happened, and the measures taken.

To fully appreciate how significant blank personal documents are to the Soviet establishment, as revealed in the last paragraph of the above quotation, we would have to imagine an equivalent theft taking place in the U.S. If the same action were taken as in the Soviet regulations, the loss would be investigated by the state police or F.B.I. and the situation would be reported to the Cabinet of the United States!

FOOTNOTES

1. Zapis Aktov Grazhdanskogo Sostoyaniya (Sbornik ofitsial'nykh materialov), Gosizdat "Yuridicheskoy literatury", Moscow, Gosizdat "Yuridicheskoy literatury", 1961, p. 15 ff.

7

Nearly half the population of the Soviet Union is subject to one further system of registration and document controls, quite apart from the PASPORT and *propiska* procedures administered by the *militsiya*, the enforcement of labor discipline overseen by the *profsoyuz* organizations, and the vital statistics archival network known as ZAGS. These persons are the male citizens of the country, specifically those between the ages of eighteen and fifty-five, plus all females who have served in the Soviet armed forces or hold reserve military status because of some particular qualifications.

This registration system is a key element in the U.S.S.R.'s juggernaut military establishment. It carries the European concept of conscription to the maximum useful limits, in that every able-bodied male is retained in standby reserve throughout his useful life, and his whereabouts at any given moment are known exactly to the military.

Peacetime conscription for young Soviets differs from the call-up which faced American men prior to 1975, in that the U.S.S.R. requires all males to register in the autumn of the year following their eighteenth birthday. There is no lottery system by which an unlucky few are drafted and the rest remain civilians. All Soviet men are enrolled in the reserve, or taken for active military service, depending on their educational qualifications and the military manpower needs of the country at the annual call-up time. Only the physically or mentally unfit are excluded from the reserve rolls, and even they must have reserve documentation which certifies their unacceptability.

The subject of Soviet military forces and how they staff their units from the pool of Russian manpower is beyond the scope of this paper. We shall investigate only the system of reserve registration as it bears upon the Soviet male in his everyday life. In particular we shall be considering the basic personal identity document which is the instrument of this registration system—the booklet entitled VOYENNYY BILET ("Military Document").

The Soviet military reserve registration system is administered by the "military commissariats" (*voyenkomaty*, an abbreviation for *voyennyy komissariat*). There are city commissariats (*gorvoyenkomaty*) for small and medium-sized cities, and raion offices (*rayvoyenkomaty*) in cities which are large enough to be divided into *rayony*, and also in rural areas. At the lowest level, military registration is done by the so-called "military roll desk" (*voyenno-uchetnyy stol*) of the village or settlement Council of Workers' Deputies.

The *voyenkomat* is staffed by active-duty military personnel, not by civilians as was the case in the American draft boards. Their numbers include military personnel officers, medical officers, and enlisted men for housekeeping and logistics. As local representatives of the Ministry of Defense they are entirely independent of the *militsiya*, ZAGS, or any other arm of the civil government. As we have already seen and will see, of course the *voyenkomat* personnel often have occasion to call on these other organs for data on individuals, and conversely to furnish such data.

The raion and city *voyenkomaty* are subordinate to oblast commissariats, which in turn come under the Military Districts *(voyennyye okruga)* that make up the internal organization of the Ministry of Defense. These districts, usually about twelve, have no relationship to civil jurisdictions such as oblasti, regions, or autonomous republics, but are instead organized according to strategic defense needs and other military considerations. They bear names like "White Sea Military District," "Don Military District," or "Maritime Military District."

As mentioned above, in the late Summer or Fall of the year after a young man has reached eighteen, he becomes subject to reserve registration. This is not a voluntary thing, whether in war or peace. Instead, the person receives a written notice *(povestka)*, by mail or messenger, from the closest *voyenkomat*. We can assume a close tie between the *voyenkomat* and the ZAGS archival system, which obviously furnishes the military the names and birth dates of young males who will become eligible in a given year. (See Rybal'chenko, *Pasportnaya Sistema*, p. 35).

After reporting to the *voyenkomat* a youth becomes technically a *"doprizyvnik,"* which means he is subject to being inducted but not yet actually called up. At this point the military establishment will direct him into one of three avenues of reserve status. If found physically or mentally unfit for any service our man will not be required to stand on the reserve registration rolls, but will carry documentary proof of his disability, as we shall see later. If physically suitable and possessing no higher education or special qualifications, he will in all likelihood be inducted soon afterward for line duty (*stroyevaya sluzhba*). As in armies in this country, a Russian lad is ordinarily sent far from home for his military service, from European Russia to the Far East, or perhaps to East Germany, etc. If our specimen has more than ordinary abilities, and is enrolled in or ear-marked for higher education, he will probably be deferred from service in the enlisted ranks, but will perform the Soviet equivalent of ROTC training in the university, *tekhnikum* or other school in which he studies. Upon graduation he will become a part of the officer reserve, for life.

Most conscripts spend two or three years in the active ranks of the army, fleet or air force. This type of service is known as "*srochnaya sluzhba*" or "fixed service". These common soldiers and seamen are usually discharged in the late Autumn, provided with a train ticket and a discharge-travel paper (*PROKHODNOYE SVIDETEL'STVO*) which directs the bearer to return to his home area by a given date. (It is an ironic coincidence that the title of this release document should be the same as that of a paper issued in Tsarist times to persons exiled to Siberia.)

Many demobilized soldiers take this opportunity to try and break away from their past civilian lives in rural areas, by simply getting off the train in Moscow or some other large city and attempting to find work and housing. A few succeeded in the face of the determined campaign of the *militsiya* and other organs mentioned in earlier sections.

Wherever the new civilian settles he must report immediately to the nearest *voyenkomat* or military roll desk with this discharge paper. There he is issued his Military Reserve Document, which he must henceforth carry on his person (along with the PASPORT) for the rest of his life.

This booklet, the VOYENNYY BILET, is an item of great significance in the life of its bearer, to an extent that can in no way be equated with the possession of a draft-status card in non-Communist countries. In its own way the booklet is of equal importance to the PASPORT, and its loss is just as serious a misdemeanor, but the consequent penalties are levied by different authorities.

The "Great Soviet Encyclopedia" provides a concise official description of the *VOYENNYY BILET:*

In the USSR a document issued by the military commissariat at the place of residence of every man liable for military service, after release from military service into the reserve, or after assignment to the reserve upon (by) passing regular call-up. In addition to military roll data, other information is given in the voyenyy bilet: concerning call-up to actual service; performance of service in the ranks of the Soviet Army or Fleet; performing musters and training periods; on medical examinations; on call-up at mobilization in war-time. Als in the v.b. are the rules of the rolls for militarily-liable persons, the knowledge and fulfillment of which are obligatory for the holder of the document.[1]

From the physical standpoint the VOYENNYY BI-

LET has always been a distinctive document; traditionally it has had a bright red leatherette cover with black
title. Until the early 1960s the booklet was somewhat
smaller in page dimensions than the PASPORT, but
contained many more pages than that document. The
pages were printed on watermarked stock, but no underprinting or other fancy artwork or special type
faces were used. Indeed, the BILET was characterized
by rather slipshod printing by most standards. It appeared that some editions were printed in local *tipogra-
fii*, perhaps by order of a military district rather than
the Ministry of Defense itself. The writer has seen two-
language versions of the VOYENNYY BILET, used in
the three Baltic republics, Estonia, Latvia and Lithua-
nia, but no other two-language exemplars from any
other area of the Soviet Union. Booklets issued even in
exotic places like Armenia and Georgia were ordinary
Russian-only editions.

Beginning about 1963 an entirely new format was introduced. This new booklet is almost identical in size
of pages with the PASPORT, and shows unmistakably
that it is a GOZNAK-produced effort, even if one does
not read the imprint of that establishment on the last
page.

A page-by-page look at our sample copy of the latest
VOYENNYY BILET will provide a fairly representative
picture of the controls which this document exerts
over the life of its bearer, for the holder of this one
seems to have had a service and reserve history typical
of most average Soviet men born since the 1920s.

The exemplar illustrated in the next several Figures
is of the new type. Its cover shows the seal of the
U.S.S.R. and the letters S.S.S.R. in hollow type face.
Below are the title, also in hollow letters, and below

that the words *"Ministerstvo Oborony"* (Ministry of Defense). The earlier, smaller editions contained only a five-pointed star between the letters S.S.S.R., and all their lettering was in solid type. (See Figure 16.)

All the pages of this exemplar are numbered at the top of the page with the numbers enclosed in squares; however, the inside cover pages at the beginning and end are left unnumbered, although the first one is the title page and the most important data page in the document. It will be noted that all pages except the cover pages are also underprinted with a large hollow star enclosing a hammer and sickle.

Our sample has a serial consisting of a two-letter prefix (in this case NM), followed by a six-digit number. Previous editions usually had a single letter in the prefix; e.g., an L or G. This prefix is printed in nineteen places in the sample document, thus assuring that no page spread is without it on at least one side.

The title-page text calls for the last name, then the first name, and below that the patronymic of the bearer. Next is a line for day, month and year of birth. The next three lines require the exact full name of the issuing authority, here the Timiryazevskiy *rayvoyenkomat* of the city of Moscow. The document was issued on 2 November 1963 and signed by the military commissar.

Numbered page one gives considerable personal data on the civil background of the bearer, in seven entry spaces which call for: full designation of birthplace, ethnic nationality, Communist Party status and Komsomol membership, education, basic profession, and marital status. From the data entered here we see that our man was born in a station in Arkhangel'skaya oblast, is of Great Russian origin, is not a party or Komso-

Figure 16

mol member, completed nine years of schooling, is a repair mechanic by trade, and is divorced. This page provides about the same detailed thumbnail sketch of the bearer as is entered in the PASPORT, but it is intended here for the information and use of military authorities rather than the police. (See Figure 17.)

Pages two through nine contain basic data concerning call-up and assignment of the bearer, under the heading "II. Relationship to Military Service." Entry 8 indicates that our man was declared fit for line duty by the Stalin *rayvoyenkomat* of the city of Groznyy and sent to a military unit on 25 July 1951. Entry 9, left blank here, would have been filled out if the bearer had been assigned directly to the reserve rather than being drafted. Entries 10 and 11 would be used for later call-ups from the reserve to active duty. Entry 12 shows that our bearer was demobilized after three years service, on the basis of an order of the Ministry of Defense No. 160, dated 8 September 1954. These orders are annual affairs, issued each Autumn to release a given number of conscripts (which will be balanced off against the new group of men just drafted). Note that the entry states that the bearer is released into the reserve and "directed to return to his place of permanent residence and stand on the rolls." (Figure 18.)

Entries 13 and 14 are used for release of regular army personnel *(sverkhsrochniki)* into the reserve. (Figure 18.)

Item 15, page four, lists our man's service in specific units with the dates of assignments. From July 1951 to April 1952 he was a rifleman *(strelok)*; from April 1952 until March 1953 he was a student in courses for officer training (apparently unsuccessfully). His final assignment, until December 1954, was as a senior clerk of a supply unit. (Figure 19.)

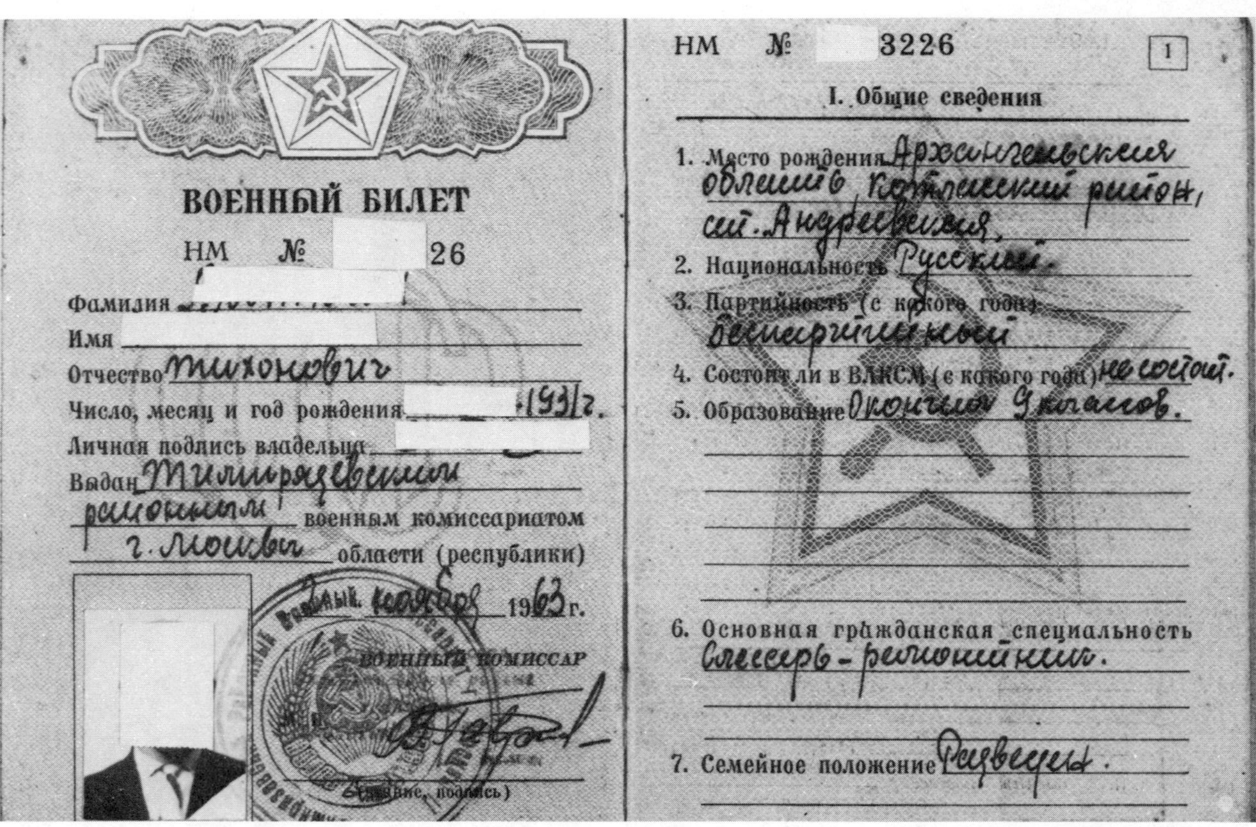

Figure 17

Figure 18

| 4 | 15. Прохождение действительной военной службы | | |

Наименование воинской части	Должность и воинское звание по штату	Дата зачисления в часть и № приказа	Дата исключения из части и № приказа
		июль 1951	апрель 1952
		апрель 1952	март 1953
			декабрь 1954

Наименование воинской части	Должность и воинское звание по штату	Дата зачисления в часть и № приказа	Дата исключения из части и № приказа

16. Заключение командования части об использовании в военное время: _____

Figure 19

Entries 17 (Performance of Service in Wartime), page 6, and 18 (Participation in Battles, Campaigns, Partisan Units and Commando Battalions), page seven, have understandably been left empty in our sample BILET, since the USSR was not at war in the period involved. However, Entry 8 is filled out, showing that the bearer took the military oath on 16 September 1951, in the unit to which he had been assigned upon call-up. This is a practice which differs from the swearing-in process in the United States, where recruits take the oath in a group at the induction center or even earlier, in a recruiting office. (Figure 20.)

Entry 20 lists the bearer's military title and specialty simply as "private" (*ryadovoy*). Item 21 shows that he earned no medals, citations or money awards; and Entry 22 affirms that he has no wounds.

Section III, "Arms and Technical Equipment" indicates no such gear issued to our subject as a reservist. (See Figure 21.)

Section IV, "Service in the Reserve", describes our bearer as being in roll category I, Roll Group SA (Soviet Army), and of the enlisted reserve (*soldatskiy sostav*). Item 27, page 12, shows his military roll specialty and his own qualification, as "riflemen" and "rifleman" respectively. (Figure 22.)

Pages thirteen through fifteen contain spaces for recording performance of training musters (*uchebnyye sbory*). The bearer apparently never participated in such activity.

Pages sixteen through eighteen are reserved for notations concerning medical examinations and inoculations. These are also blank in our exemplar. (Figure 23.) Pages nineteen through twenty-two are for entries recording issuance and handing back of the Mobilization

Figure 20

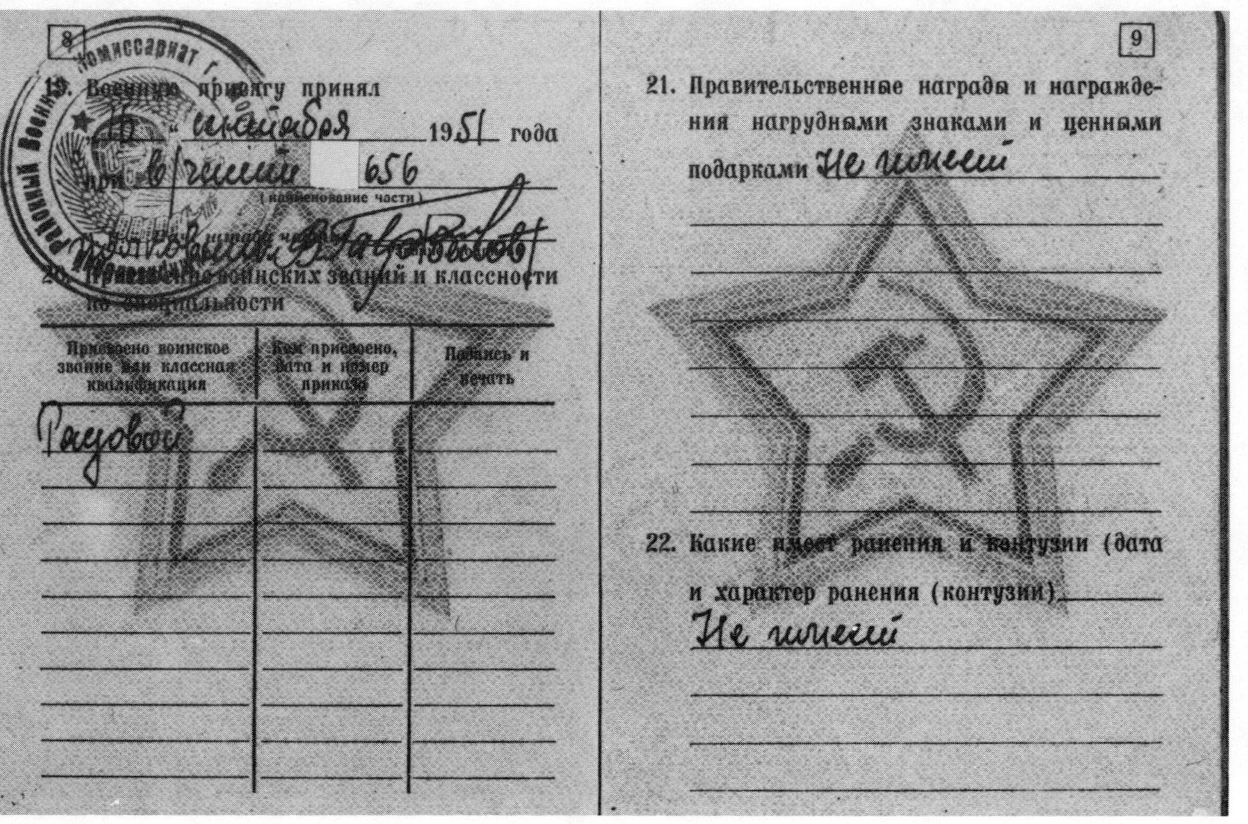

Figure 20 continued

Figure 21

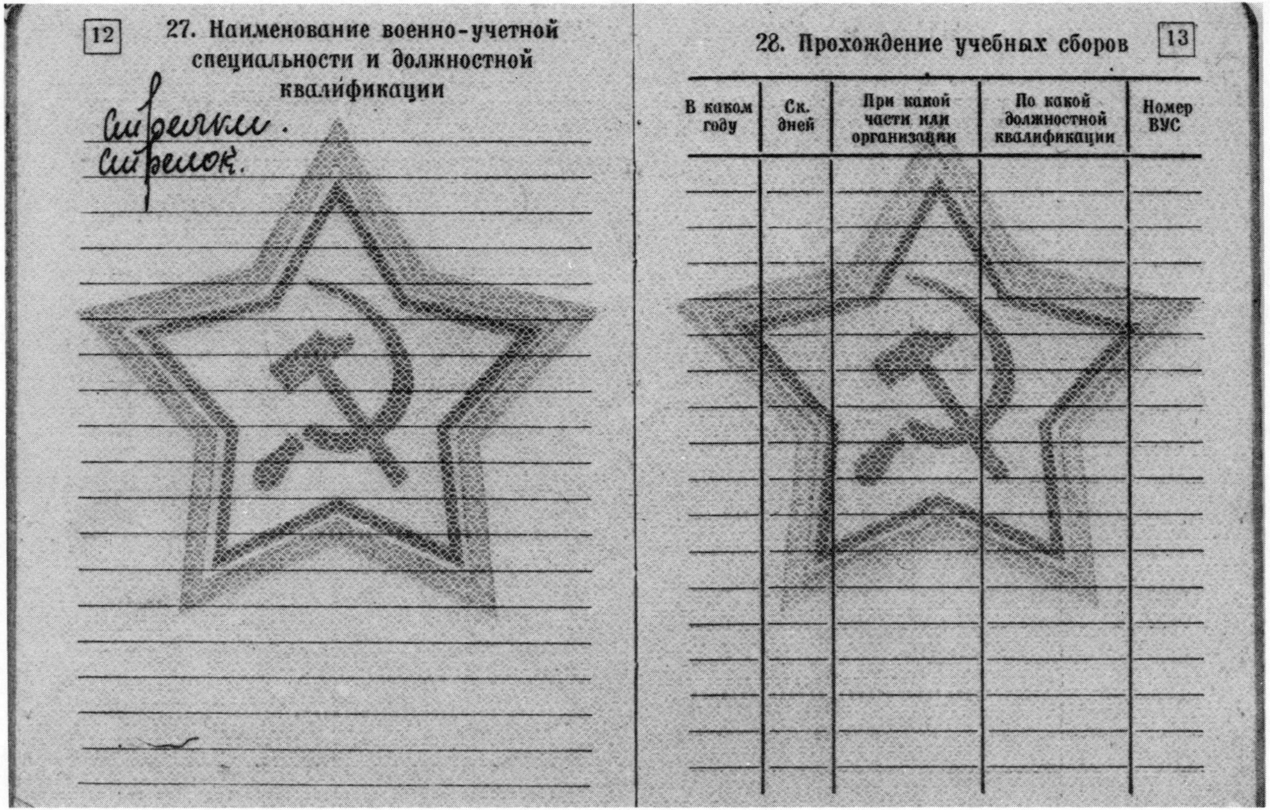

12

27. Наименование военно-учетной специальности и должностной квалификации

Стрелки.
Стрелок.

28. Прохождение учебных сборов

13

В каком году	Ск. дней	При какой части или организации	По какой должностной квалификации	Номер ВУС

Figure 22

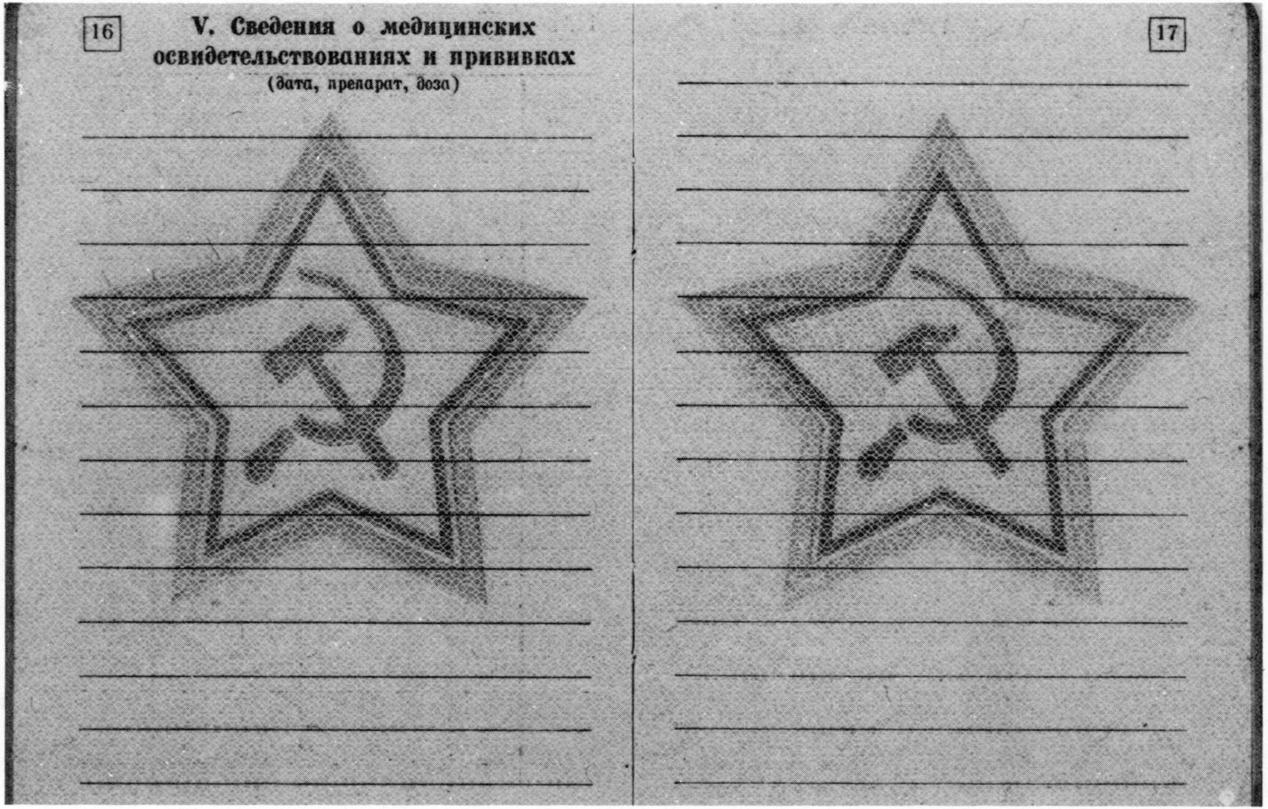

Figure 23

Order *(MOBILIZATSIONNOYE PREDPISANIYE)*, a significant document which is used only in the event of mass call-up of reserves in time of national emergency. This rare item has apparently never been used on any large scale since World War II, but *it is obvious from Section VI that the Soviet government is always prepared for mobilization.* (Figures 24, 25.)

Section VII, "Special Remarks," is a catch-all category for any type of descriptive data on the bearer for which no other specific heading exists in the VOYENNYY BILET. Our sample document contains a very significant entry here, a stamped cachet of the 16th *militsiya* division in Moscow, stating that the bearer had been issued a new PASPORT on 21 November 1964. Up until the late 1960s no such notation was ever seen in the West in a Military Reserve Booklet. It shows that the police registration system now requires that male citizens produce not only PASPORT and other civil papers in the course of PASPORT issue, but also the VOYENNYY BILET. We shall discuss this further in our examination of the regulations concerning use of the document (Figure 25.)

Pages 26 through 31 provide space for the chief function of this booklet, namely to record proof of the bearer's standing on the reserve rolls of a *voyenkomat* or military rolls desk. As in earlier printings of the document, these pages are divided in the middle, the left half of each being reserved for cachets showing the holder taken on the rolls, and the right side for release from the rolls. These stamps have traditionally been square, simple affairs listing the office taking action, the date, and validated by the signature of the "official of the 4th section" (which handles enlisted reserve rolls). The cachet in the sample shows that the bearer

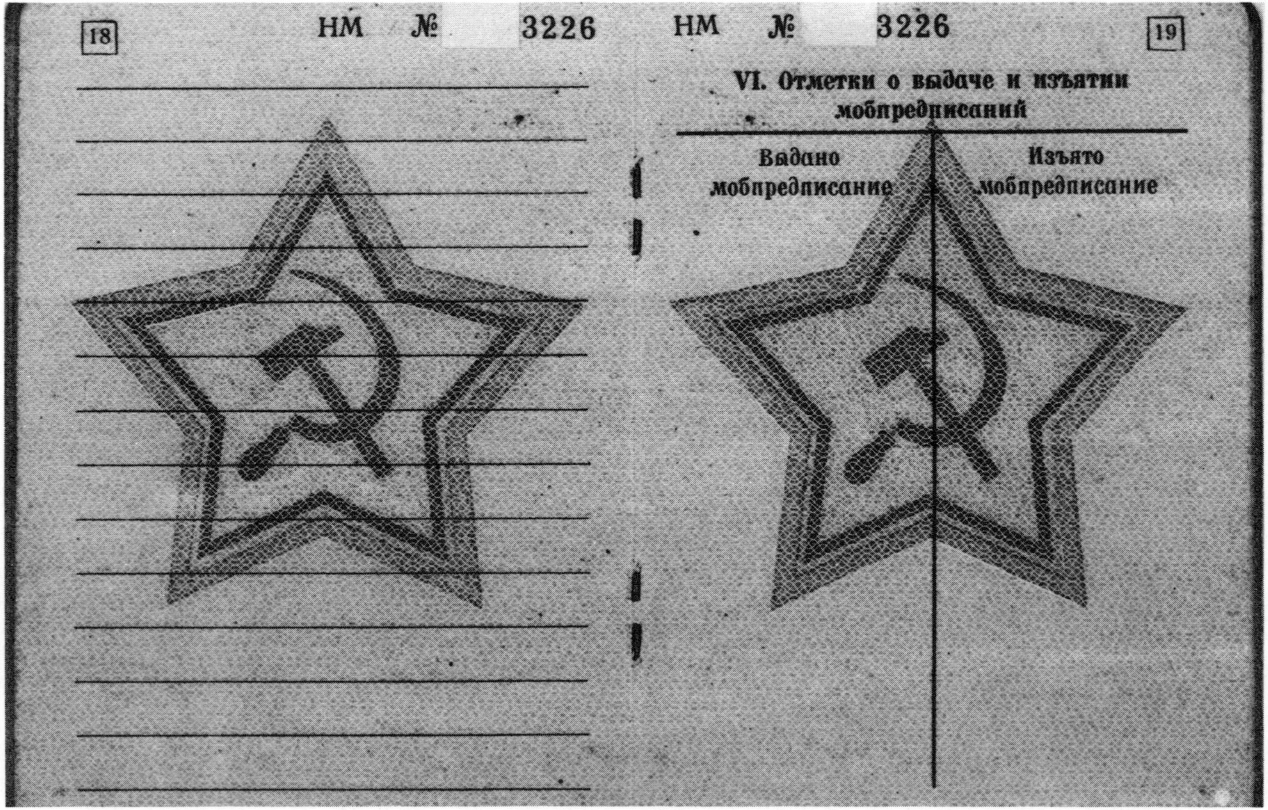

НМ № 3226
НМ № 3226
VI. Отметки о выдаче и изъятии
мобпредписаний
Выдано
мобпредписание
Изъято
мобпредписание

Figure 24

22
НМ № 3226
ВЫдано
мобпредписание
Изъято
мобпредписание
НМ № 3226
23
VII. Особые отметки
Выдан паспорт серии XXV-СА № 948
от „21" ноября 1964 г.
16 отделением милиции г. Москвы

Figure 25

was taken on the rolls at the Timiryazevskiy *rayvoy-enkomat* on 11 May 1963. (Figure 26.)

The final set of entries in this new edition of the Reserve Booklet represent a basic departure from military practice prior to the early 1960s. In the past any male found physically or otherwise medically unfit for any military service did not carry a VOYENNYY BILET. Instead, such a person was issued a simple card-like document with the jaw-breaking title SVIDETEL'STVO OB OSVOBOZHDENII OT VOINSKOY OBYAZANNOSTI (Certificate of Exemption from Military Obligation). Understandably, generations of Russian men referred to this critical paper simply as *"bely bilet"* ("white ticket", as distinct from the red-covered Reserve Booklet). The printed text of this earlier document was essentially the same as the wording in Section IX, Entry 29 of the new Booklet, which is entitled "Notes Concerning Exemption from Military Obligation."

Our bearer is unusual in that his booklet does contain an exemption entry in this Section, as follows:

Pronounced unfit for military service, with exclusion from the rolls, according to Chapter I, Article 4 of the (military) Table of Infirmities *(raspisaniye bolezney)*, promulgated by order of the Ministry of Defense No. ...7 December 1961, and excluded from the rolls by a physicians' commission at the Timiryazevskiiy rayvoyenkomat on 2 November 1963.

It will be noted that this date of exclusion from the rolls is identical with the issuance date of the document, on the title page (Figure 27). This means that the bearer was given this new type VOYENNYY BILET upon the occasion of his being examined by the voy-

148

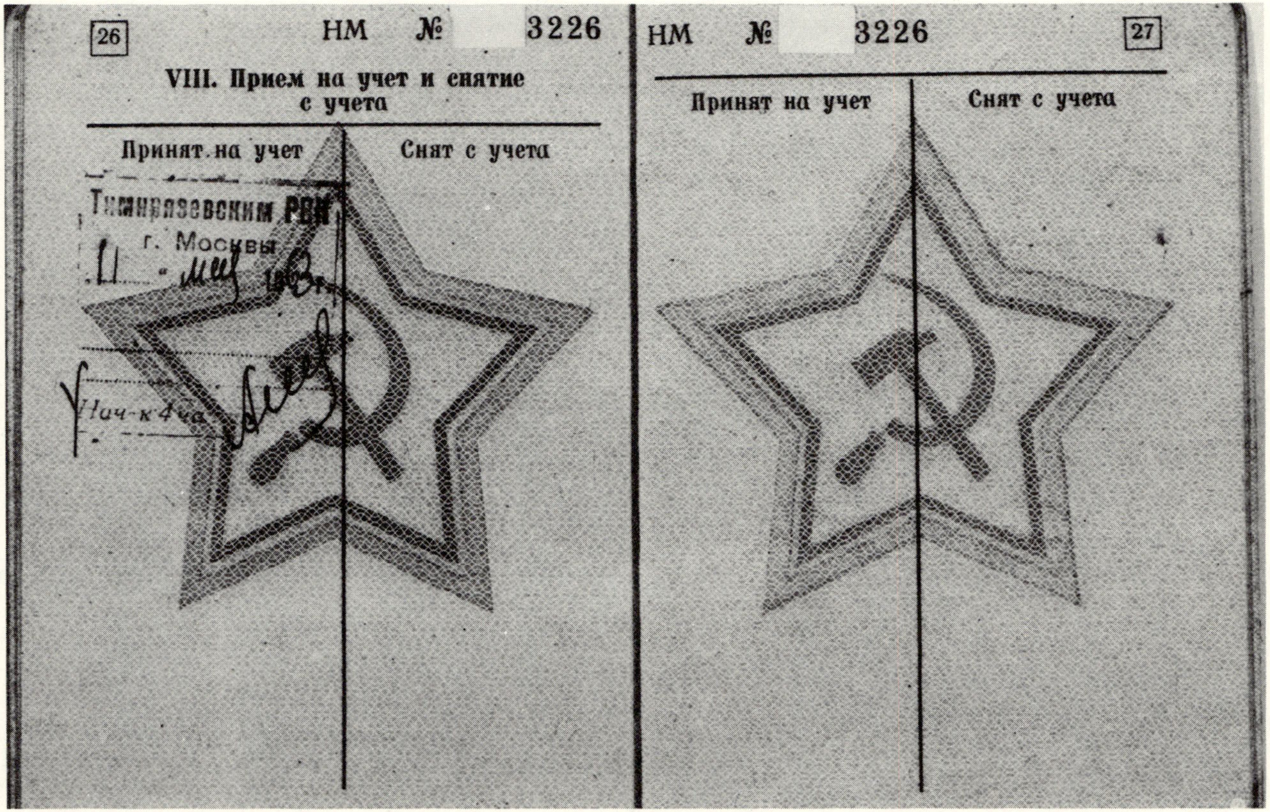
26
НМ № 3226
VIII. Прием на учет и снятие с учета
Принят на учет
Снят с учета
Тимирязевским РВК
г. Москвы
НМ № 3226
27
Принят на учет
Снят с учета

Figure 26

32 | IX. Отметки об освобождении
от воинской обязанности | 33

29. _____ ноября 19 63 г. врачебной комиссией при _______ рай (гор) военкомате ________ области (края, республики) признан негодным к военной службе с исключением с учета по гр. __ ст. 4 расписания болезней, объявленного приказом МО СССР № ________ от ________ 19 6 г., исключен с воинского учета.

Личная подпись владельца билета _______

М. П. Военный комиссар _______ (звание, подпись)

______ ноября ____ 19 68 г.

31. Подлежит переосвидетельствованию

"____"________ 19 ___ г.

Личная подпись владельца билета _______

М. П. Военный комиссар _______ (звание, подпись)

32. "____"________ 19 ___ г. врачебной комиссией при _______ рай (гор) военкомате ________ области (края, республики) признан негодным к военной службе с исключением с учета по гр. ___ ст. ___ расписания болезней, объявленного приказом МО СССР № ________ от "____"________ 19 ___ г., исключен с воинского учета.

М. П. Военный комиссар _______ (звание, подпись)

33. Подлежит переосвидетельствованию

"____"________ 19 ___ г.

Личная подпись владельца билета _______

М. П. Военный комиссар _______ (звание, подпись)

34. Исключен с воинского учета

"____"________ 19 ___ г.

за достижением предельного возраста состояния в запасе.

М. П. Военный комиссар _______ (звание, подпись)

Figure 27

enkomat doctors, and presumably his earlier booklet was taken from him. We can probably assume then that such an exchange of documents has taken place by now throughout the USSR, and that all *draft-age men* now carry this new type, whether they are fit for service or not (since Entry 29 now takes the place of the old exemption certificate).

Entry 30 declares that the bearer is subject to re-examination by physicians in November 1968, i.e., five years hence.

Entry 34 (left blank here) is interesting in that no such entry appeared in earlier versions of the VOYEN-NYY BILET. It contains the notation that the bearer has been taken from the rolls upon attaining "the limiting age for standing in the reserve." In the past this age has been fifty-five, and presumably this is still true. (Figure 27.)

Three of the remaining four pages of the Reserve Booklet shown in our illustrations contain printed "regulations operative in relation to the voyennyy bilet", Section X. (See Figure 28.) These rules are of such critical significance to all male citizens of the Soviet Union, and afford so unusual an insight into a major system of control over the individual, that a full translation of them for the non-Russian reader seems in order:

1. The voyennyy bilet is the sole document certifying the identity of sergeants, senior sergeants and seamen on actual service, and defines the relationship of the militarily-liable person to military service in the reserve of the Armed Forces.
2. The v.b. is of unlimited validity, and is issued by the military commissariat only once, at the call-up of citizens to active military service.

151

НМ № 3226

Х. ПРАВИЛА,
действующие в отношении военного билета

1. Военный билет является единым документом, удостоверяющим личность сержанта, старшины, солдата и матроса, состоящих на действительной военной службе, и определяет отношение военнообязанного к военной службе в запасе Вооруженных Сил.

2. Военный билет является бессрочным, выдается военным комиссариатом один раз в момент призыва граждан на действительную военную службу.

3. Сержанты, старшины, солдаты и матросы обязаны бережно хранить военный билет, постоянно иметь его при себе, следить за своевременным и точным внесением изменений и предъявлять его соответствующим должностным лицам.

   Военный билет может быть сдан под расписку в штаб воинской части или учебного пункта, военный комиссариат, военно-учетный стол, судебно-следственным органам и домоуправлениям (ЖЭК). Кроме указаных выше органов, никто не имеет права отбирать военный билет.

4. Лица, уволенные с военной службы или зачисленные в запас, обязаны встать на воинский учет в установленный срок, но не позднее 3-х дней со дня прибытия к избранному месту жительства.

5. Сержанты, старшины, солдаты и матросы запаса обязаны выполнять следующие правила:

   а) состоять на воинском учете по месту жительства: в городе — в военном комиссариате, в сельской местности, а также в городе, где нет военного комиссариата, — военно-учетном столе при исполкоме местного Совета депутатов трудящихся;

   б) при перемене постоянного места жительства (или при выездах временно на срок свыше 1,5 месяца, а в служебные командировки и для лечения на срок свыше трех месяцев):

   по прибытии в город или в район другого военного комиссариата в этом же городе сдать домоуправлению (ЖЭК) вместе с паспортом и свой военный билет для оформления приема на воинский учет;

   при убытии из города или на территорию другого военного комиссариата в том же городе сдать домоуправлению (ЖЭК) военный билет для снятия с воинского учета;

   по прибытии в сельскую местность в трехдневный срок лично явиться в сельский (поселковый) Совет для принятия на воинский учет;

   при убытии в другую местность или на территорию другого сельского Совета того же района лично явиться в сельский (поселковый) Совет для снятия с воинского учета;

   в) при временных выездах на срок менее 1,5 месяца, а в служебные командировки и для лечения на срок до трех месяцев должен сообщить об этом тому учетному органу, где состоит на учете;

   г) при изменении фамилии, имени, образования, партийности, должности и места работы должен явиться в пятидневный срок в военно-учетный орган по месту состояния на учете с военным билетом и документами, подтверждающими эти изменения;

   д) при получении увечья или после перенесенного тяжелого заболевания, нарушившего трудоспособность, должен подать заявление в военный комиссариат по месту жительства для проведения переосвидетельствования;

Figure 28

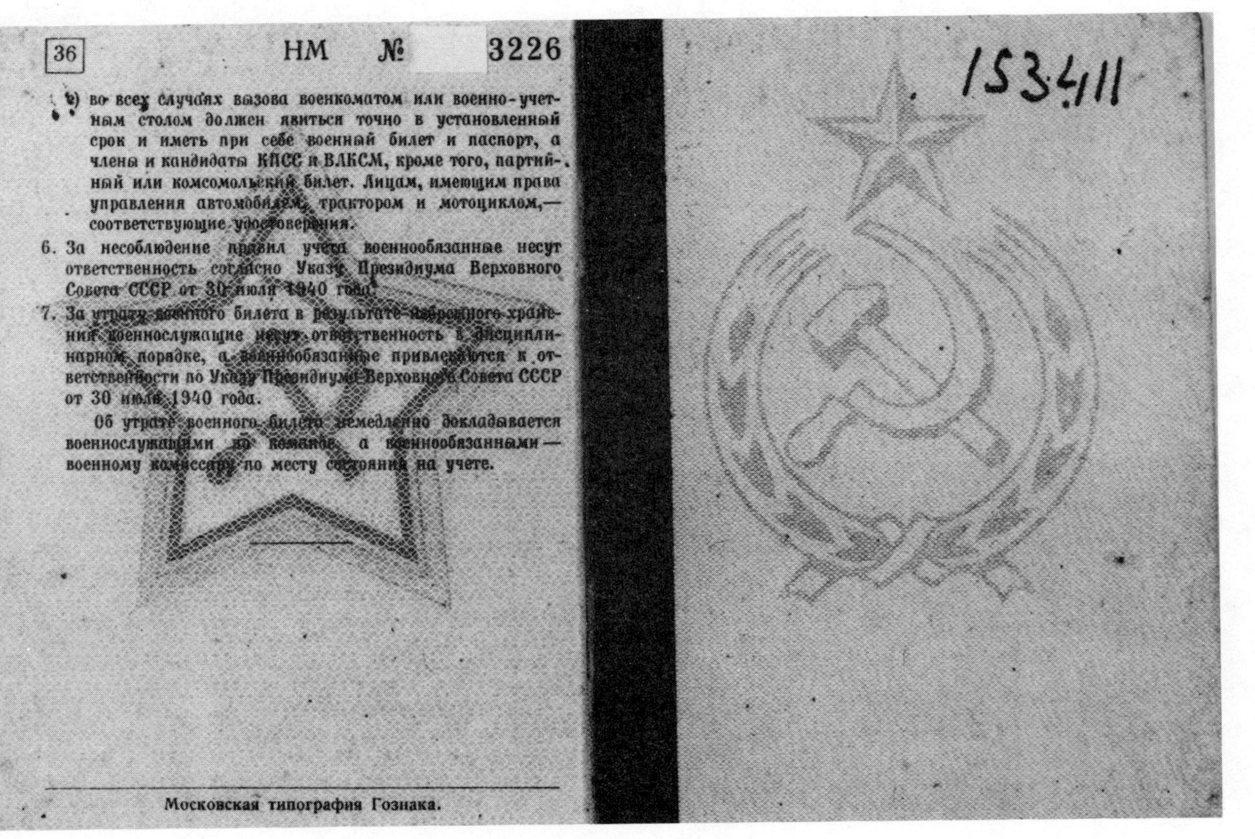

Figure 28 continued

3. Sergeants, senior sergeants, privates and seamen
are required to preserve the v.b. carefully, to have
it continually on their persons, to assure the timely
and exact entry of changes, and to present it to the
appropriate officials.

The voyennyy bilet may be handed over, against
a receipt, to the staff of a military unit or training
point, to a voyenkomat, to a military rolls desk, to
court-investigative organs or to housing directo-
ries (ZhEK). Except for the above designated organs, no one has the right to take away the
voyennyy bilet.

4. Persons released from military service, or assigned
into the reserve, are required to stand on the military draft rolls within an established period, but
not later than three days from the day of arrival at
the selected place of residence.

5. Sergeants, senior sergeants, privates and seamen
of the reserve are required to observe the following
regulations:

   a) to stand on the military rolls at the place of residence: in cities, at a voyenkomat; in a rural locality or in a city where there is no
voyenkomat, at a voyenno-uchetnyy stol (military rolls desk) of the Executive Council...

   b) Upon change of permanent residence (or on
temporary trips for periods of more than 1½
months, on official travel, and for medical
treatment for more than 3 months): upon arrival in a city, or in the raion of another voyenkomat within the same city, to yield to the
housing directorate...one's v.b. together with
the PASPORT, for the formality of being taken
on the rolls;

upon departing from a city, or to the territory of
another voyenkomat within the same city, to
yield the v.b. to the housing authority for removal from the rolls;

upon arrival in a rural locality, to appear within
3 days at the village...council to be taken on
the rolls;

upon departure to another locality, or to the territory of another village council in the same
raion, to appear personally at the village council to be taken off the rolls;

c) in case of trips for less than 1½ months, and an
official trips and for treatment for periods up to
3 months, one must make this known to the
rolls organ where he resides;

d) upon any change in last or first name, education, Party status, work status and place of
work, one must appear within 5 days at the military rolls organ at the place where he stands
on the rolls, with the voyennyy bilet and documents affirming these changes;

e) upon receiving an impairment or after pro-
longed serious illness, which breaks one's capacity to work, he must give a deposition to the
voyenkomat at his place of residence, to un-
dergo re-examination;

6. For non-observance of the regulation of the rolls,
militarily liable persons bear responsibility in accordance with the *Ukaz* of the Presidium of the Supreme Soviet USSR, of 30 July 1930.

7. For loss of the voyennyy bilet because of careless
keeping, persons on active military duty bear responsibility in disciplinary procedure, and a

militarily-liable person is subject to accountability according to the (above) *Ukaz*...Loss of the v.b. is reported to one's headquarters by active-duty persons, and to the voyenkomat where one stands on the rolls by militarily-liable persons."

The cited regulations show clearly that still another vast branch of Soviet bureaucracy is extending its empire and thereby increasing its measure of control over the individual. The Ministry of Defense has obviously yielded none of its prerogatives to any civil authority. It can require citizens to produce not only documents issued by ZAGS and components of various ministries in connection with employment, but even official papers issued by and controlled by the KGB *militsiya* and the Party itself. Of course, since all these organs serve the same masters, only the individual citizen loses anything from this continuing process of tightening of the web of control over his whereabouts and actions.

We should comment on one significant change embodied in this new edition of the Military Reserve Booklet and the procedures cited for its use. This is the stated fact that it is used not only as an identity document for those who are civilians of the reserve, but also is "...the sole document certifying the identity of sergeants, senior sergeants, privates and seamen on active military duty." This implies that the identity documents formerly carried by such persons no longer exist. These were: the *SLUZHEBNAYA KNIZHKA VOYENNO-SLUZHASHCHEGO KRASNOY ARMII* for enlisted persons on conscript status, and the *SLUZHEBNAYA KNIZHKA SVERKHSROCHNO-SLUZHASHCHEGO KRASNOY ARMII* for extended-duty non-coms. Similar booklets were carried by those serving actively in the Soviet Fleet.

The years since the end of World War II have seen the continual refinement of personal document controls, a process of plugging the loopholes through which the cunning and the resourceful might slip to evade this or that responsibility to the Communist state. Evidently the process must be about complete.

FOOTNOTES

1. Bol'shaya Sovetskaya Entsiklopediya, 1st edition, vol. 35, pp. 171–2.

8

In the seven preceding sections we have had a brief look at several areas of control over the individual Soviet citizen by means of personal identity documentation and associated registration procedures. These are by no means all the documents which play important parts in the lives of individuals in the U.S.S.R. For example, we shall only mention but not analyze the important membership booklet carried by that small, privileged minority of Soviets who are members of the Communist Party, the document called *PARTIYNYY BILET.* (See Figure 29.) There is also the similar membership booklet issued to the larger group of younger citizens who belong to the Young Communist League, the *KOMSOMOL'SKIY BILET.* We should also mention the *STUDENCHESKIY BILET,* a booklet carried by all students enrolled in higher education. This document is similar in function to the Work Booklet, but instead of listing job assignments and awards, it shows the course in which the bearer is enrolled and how good his marks are in them, on a scale of four.

After this quick introduction to the world of Commu-

Пролетарии всех стран, соединяйтесь!

КОММУНИСТИЧЕСКАЯ ПАРТИЯ СОВЕТСКОГО СОЮЗА

ПАРТИЙНЫЙ БИЛЕТ

№   12460 ✻

Фамилия

Имя и отчество *Александр Васильевич*

Год рождения *1929.*

Время вступления в партию *Декабрь-1955*

Наименование организации, выдавшей билет *Политотдел 124 Гауб. Арт.Прожск.Брп.Б.М.*

Время выдачи партбилета *16 Февраля 1956 г.*

УПЛАТА ЧЛЕНСКИХ ВЗНОСОВ 1956 год			
Месяц	Месячный заработок	Членский взнос	Подпись секретаря
Январь			
Февраль	687	6 87	
Март	687	6 87	
Апрель	687	6 87	
Май			
Июнь			
Июль			
Август			
Сентябрь			
Октябрь			
Ноябрь			
Декабрь			

Figure 29

nist preoccupation with personal documents, the reader will probably feel relieved at the thought that we in the free world are not obliged to endure such regimentation. He may also dismiss it as a purely Russian phenomenon, a quirk of the Russian predilection for things conspiratorial, something which is not necessarily characteristic of Communism elsewhere. After all, the "peoples' democracies" have shown a strong trend in recent years to independent thought in their interpretations of Marxism; perhaps outside the Communist motherland the ironhanded controls we have been describing just are not needed.

For those who may entertain this idea we shall present some dismaying evidence to the contrary. Of course we can only hint here at the extent of document controls in the rest of the Communist world; a full book could be written *(and it should be!)* about this subject as it pertains to each Communist country. Suffice it here to reproduce only the basic identity document of each (the local equivalent of the Soviet PASPORT), and to comment briefly on the similarities of procedure and intent.

POLISH PEOPLE'S REPUBLIC

From the standpoint of personal identity papers a Russian would feel quite at home in Poland. Every citizen there is also in possession of a basic identity booklet, almost precisely the equivalent in size and format of the Soviet PASPORT, entitled *DOWOD OSOBISTY*. The name signifies approximately "Certificate of Identity".

161

Figure 30

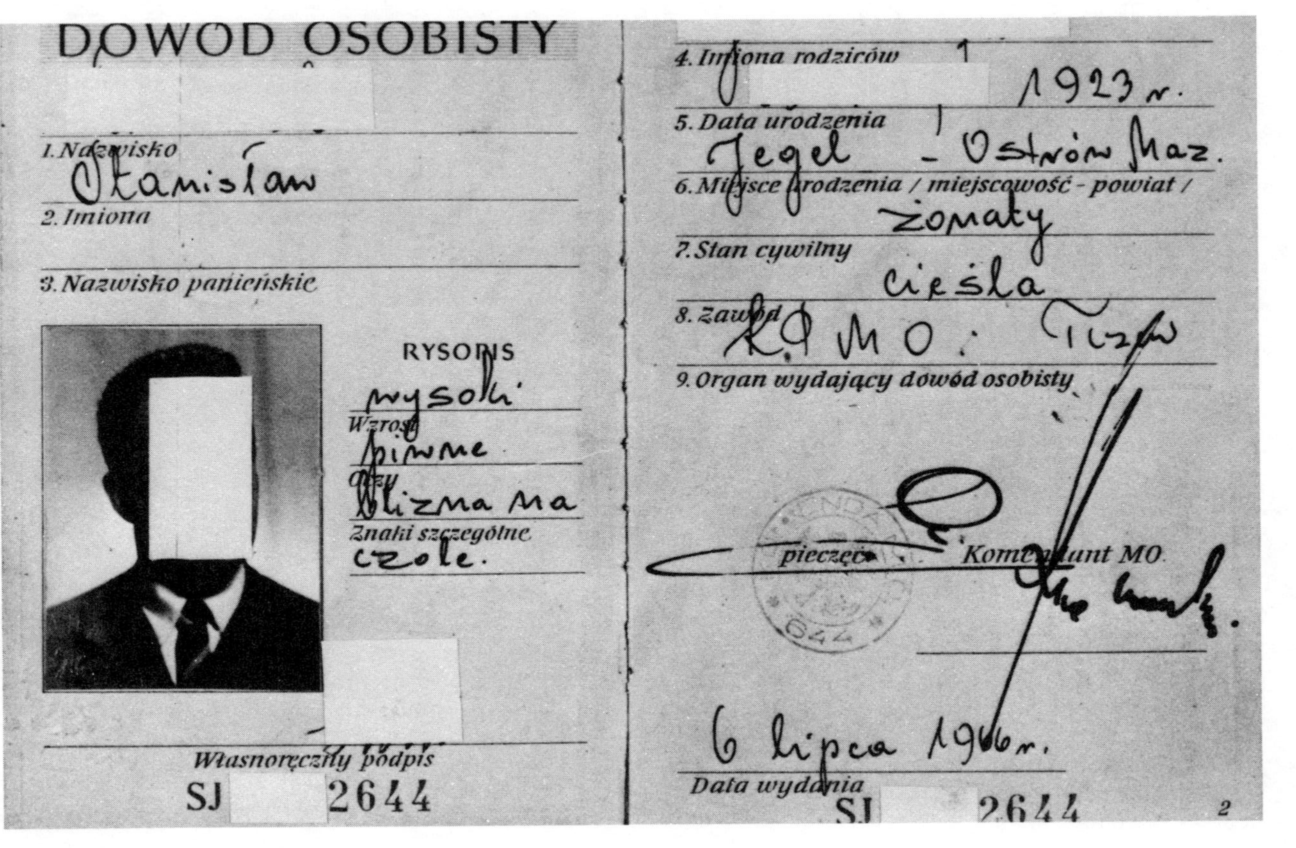

Figure 30 continued

The *DOWOD OSOBISTY* has some features which are characteristically Central European, a heritage of Poland's Austro-Hungarian past. The cover material and the cover text layout with the Polish eagle, the title printing on the first page, and the bearer's physical description are all more typically Germanic than Slavic. But in most other respects the booklet is a virtual Polish translation of the PASPORT. The bearer's photo is validated by a small circular embossed "dry seal" just as in the Soviet Counterpart, and the general text layout of the first page spread is much like that of the PASPORT, except for the lines for the bearer's description. (Figure 30.)

Page three of the *DOWOD OSOBISTY* is again a straightaway copy of the page in the PASPORT which lists the dependent children of the bearer, through age fifteen. (Figure 31.)

Pages four through eight are the functional equivalents of the residence registration *(propiska)* pages of the Soviet document, with printed spaces for registration and de-registration of residence. On the other hand, pages nine and ten are specifically reserved for employment entries, which are made by small stamped cachets very like the "hired" and "released" ones in the "Special Remarks" pages of the PASPORT. The *DOWOD OSOBISTY* has three pages entitled simply "Notes" for entry of other types of remarks. (Figure 32.)

The final page of the Polish identity booklet contains printed instructions very similar to those in the corresponding page of the PASPORT. (Figure 33.)

It will be noted that eight of the fourteen pages of the *DOWOD OSOBISTY* contain a printed serial, in such a manner that each unbound page spread contains this

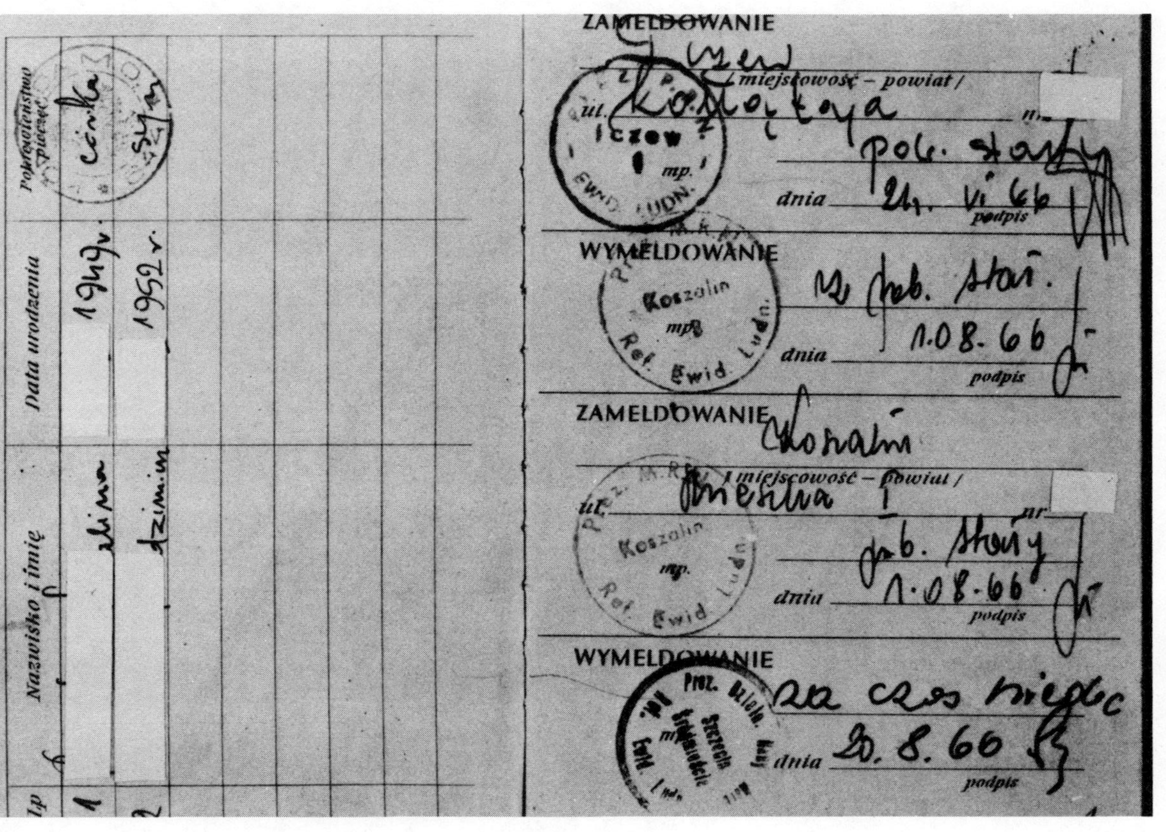

Figure 31

Figure 32

Adnotacje

POUCZENIE

1. Dowód osobisty jest jedynym dokumentem stwierdzającym tożsamość osoby.
2. Dowód osobisty należy przechowywać starannie i zabezpieczyć przed zniszczeniem, zgubieniem oraz kradzieżą.
3. W przypadku utraty dowodu osobistego bądź znalezienia własnego dowodu zgłoszonego jako utracony należy bezzwłocznie zawiadomić o tym najbliższy organ MO.
4. W przypadku zmiany nazwiska lub imienia, uszkodzenia dowodu osobistego w stopniu utrudniającym posługiwanie się nim lub w przypadku wyczerpania się miejsca na dokonywanie nowych wpisów, posiadacz dowodu osobistego obowiązany jest dokonać jego wymiany.
5. Wpisy i skreślenia w dowodzie osobistym mogą być dokonywane tylko przez uprawnione organy.
6. Nieprzestrzeganie obowiązujących przepisów o dowodach osobistych pociąga za sobą odpowiedzialność karną przewidzianą w dekrecie z dnia 22 października 1951 r. o dowodach osobistych.

SJ 2644

SJ 2644

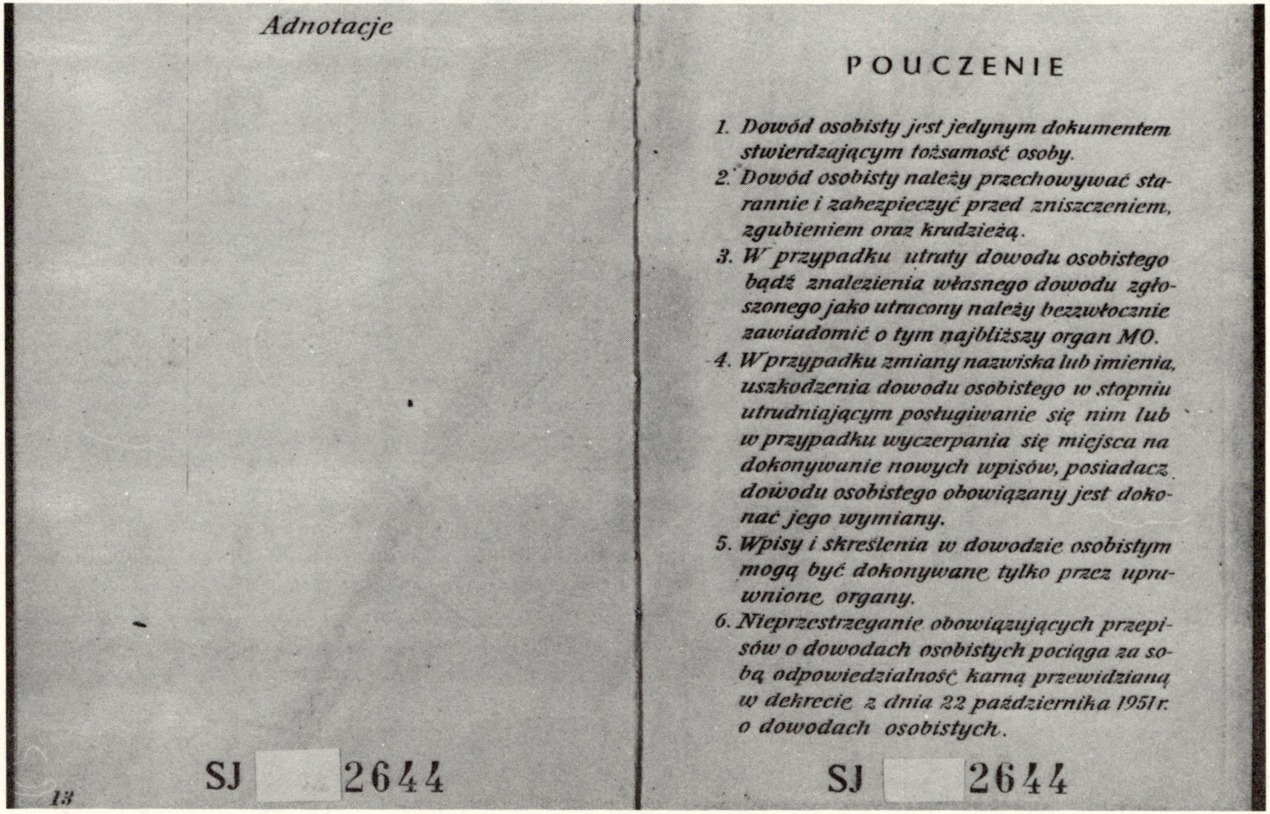

Figure 33

identification on at least one side. Following the scheme of the Soviet PASPORT this serial consists of a two-letter prefix followed by an Arabic number.

CZECHOSLOVAK SOCIALIST REPUBLIC

To the South in Czechoslovakia we find again that all adults are in possession of a basic identity booklet, entitled *OBCANSKY PRUKAZ*. To be strictly accurate we should note that in Slovak-speaking Eastern parts of the country there is a separate edition printed in Slovak. Superficially the document differs considerably from the Russian PASPORT, except for page size. The plastic cover is bright red, and the booklet, as with all satellite country identity papers, is stitched together rather than stapled. The bearer's photo is on the second page rather than the first, and is affixed by two metal grommets in a manner typical of German documentation. At a glance the page layouts seem also quite un-Soviet.

But from the standpoint of content and functions the entries in the *OBCANSKY PRUKAZ* faithfully parallel those of the PASPORT, even though four pages are used to record essentially the same data as is given in two pages of the Soviet document. Perhaps the most different feature is the provision of two pages for extension of the validity of the booklet.

The "Important Remarks" pages (14 and 15) correspond to the "Special Remarks" pages of the PASPORT in function, but spell out the intended uses—for recording marriage, divorce, stay in border areas, etc.—in printed text at the top of each page.

The serial number in the *OBCANSKY PRUKAZ* contains three elements as does the PASPORT, but the order is different. In the Czech document the six-digit Arabic number comes first, then the two-letter series followed by a two-digit suffix. This serial number appears on every page. (See Figures 34 through 37.)

HUNGARIAN PEOPLE'S REPUBLIC

Hungary may be a complete linguistic anomaly, a Finno-Ugric island surrounded by largely Slavic neighbors with whom it shares little in common ethnically, but its system of identity documentation shows the Soviet inspiration and influence just as strongly as those in the "little Slavic brother" states of Poland and Czechoslovakia. The key identity document is entitled SZEMELYI IGAZOLVANY, which means approximately "Personal Certificate".

As in the Czech identity booklet, the Hungarian one contains all the data sections found in the Soviet PASPORT, usually at greater length, and in somewhat different order. Like all the Central European identity documents the *SZEMELYI IGAZOLVANY* is sewn together rather than crudely stapled as is the PASPORT. The pagination is unusual, in that the first page (inside front cover) is considered as page two, and the final one (inside rear cover) is left unnumbered. As in all the Communist identity booklets we see the serial, consist-

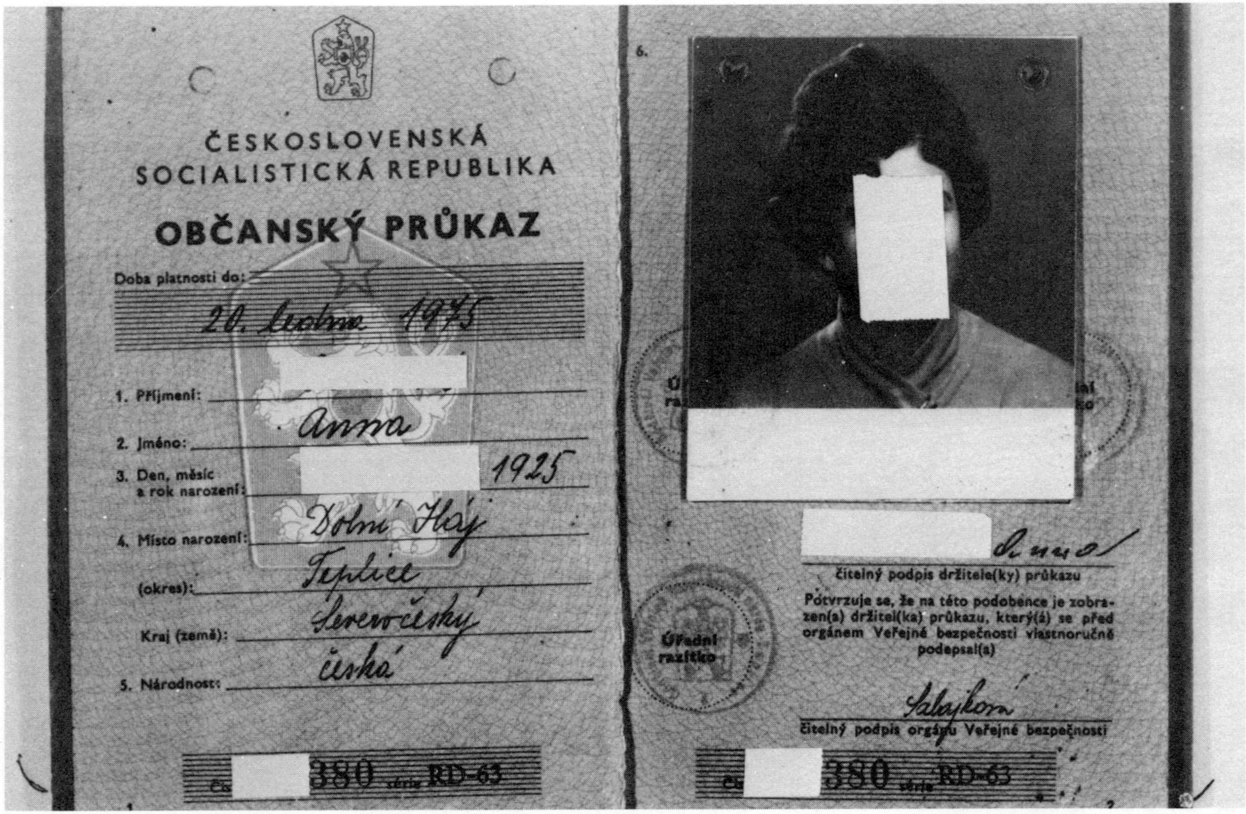

ČESKOSLOVENSKÁ
SOCIALISTICKÁ REPUBLIKA

OBČANSKÝ PRŮKAZ

Doba platnosti do:

20. února 1975

1. Příjmení:

2. Jméno: Anna

3. Den, měsíc
a rok narození: 1925

4. Místo narození: Dolní Háj

(okres): Teplice

Kraj (země): Severočeský

5. Národnost: česká

6.

čitelný podpis držitele(ky) průkazu

Potvrzuje se, že na této podobence je zobra-
zen(a) držitel(ka) průkazu, který(á) se před
orgánem Veřejné bezpečnosti vlastnoručně
podepsal(a)

Úřední
razítko

čitelný podpis orgánu Veřejné bezpečnosti

čs. 380 série RD-63

čs. 380 série RD-63

Figure 34

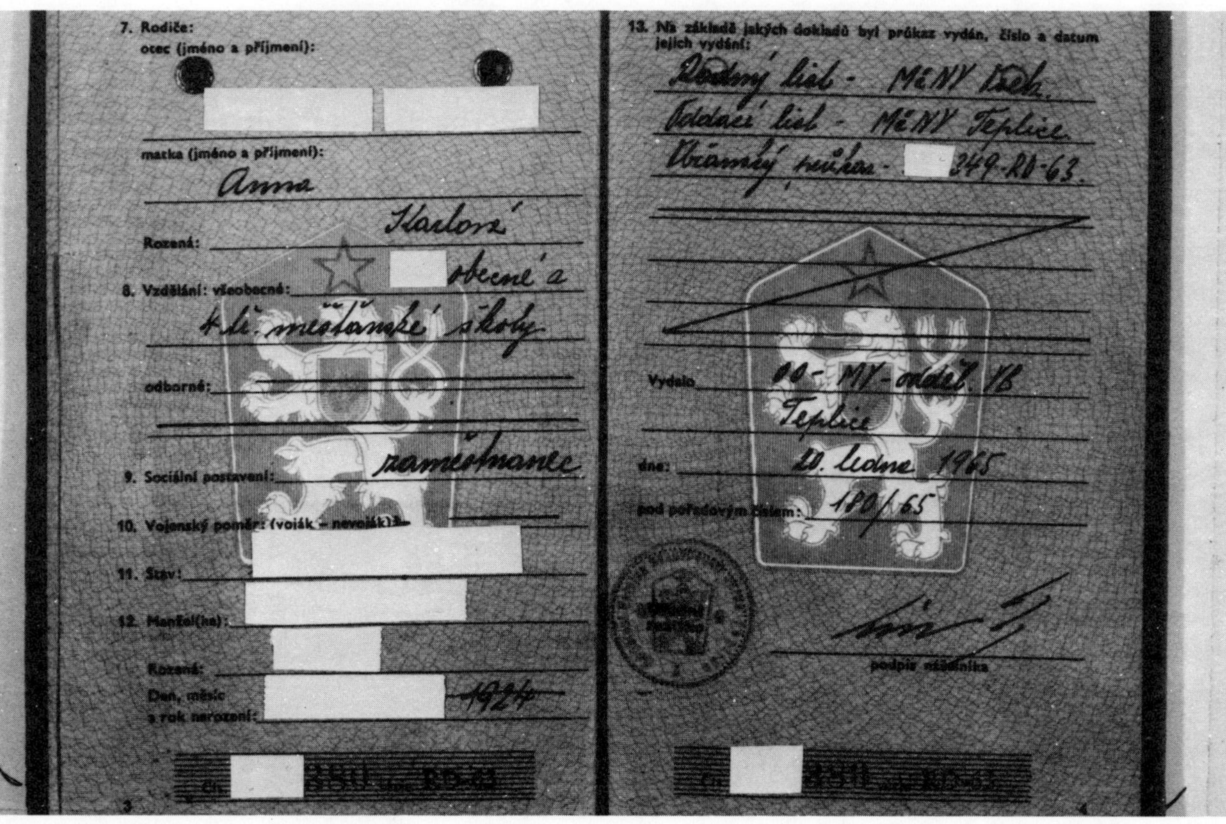

Figure 34 continued

14.
Děti mladší 15 let:
Pol. čís.
Příjmení a jméno
Rodinný poměr
Děti mladší 15 let:
Den, měsíc, rok a místo narození
Číslo rodného listu, kým a kdy byl vydán
380 série RD-63
380 série RD-63

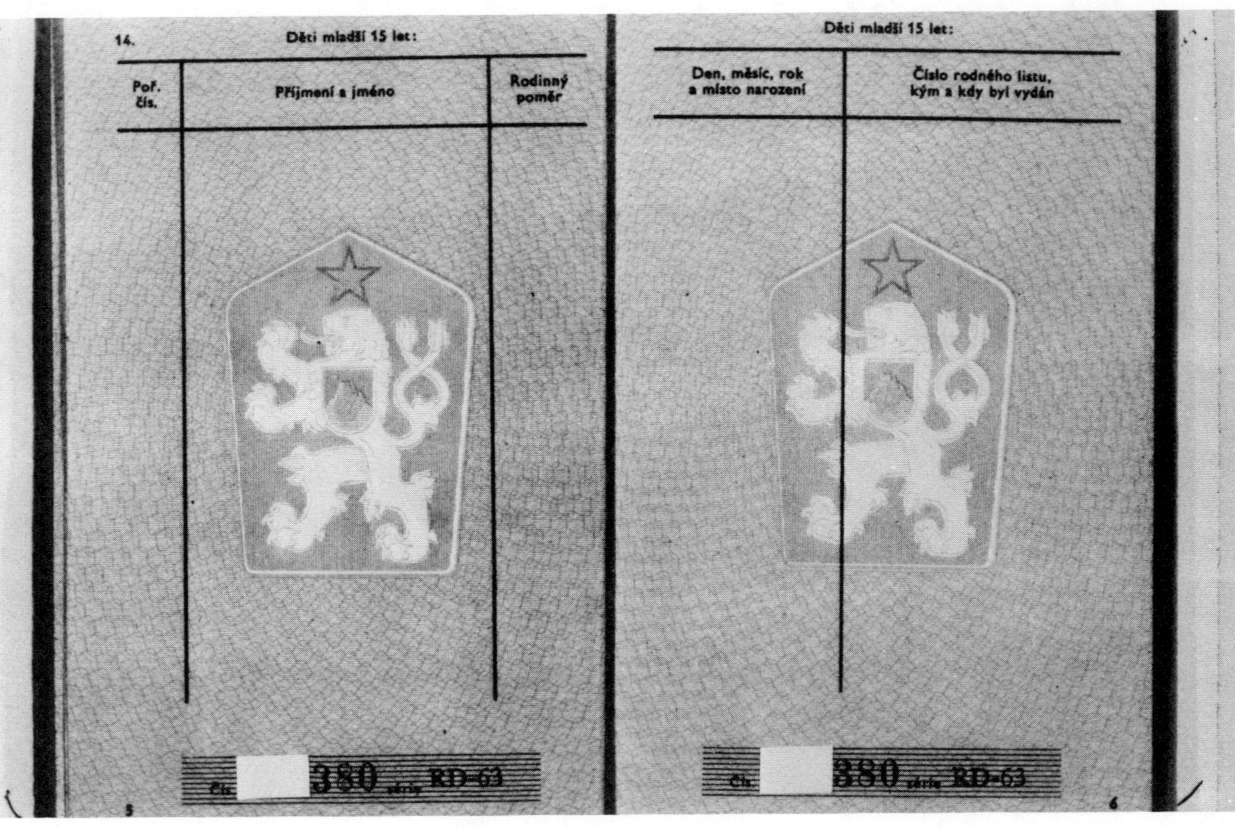

Figure 35

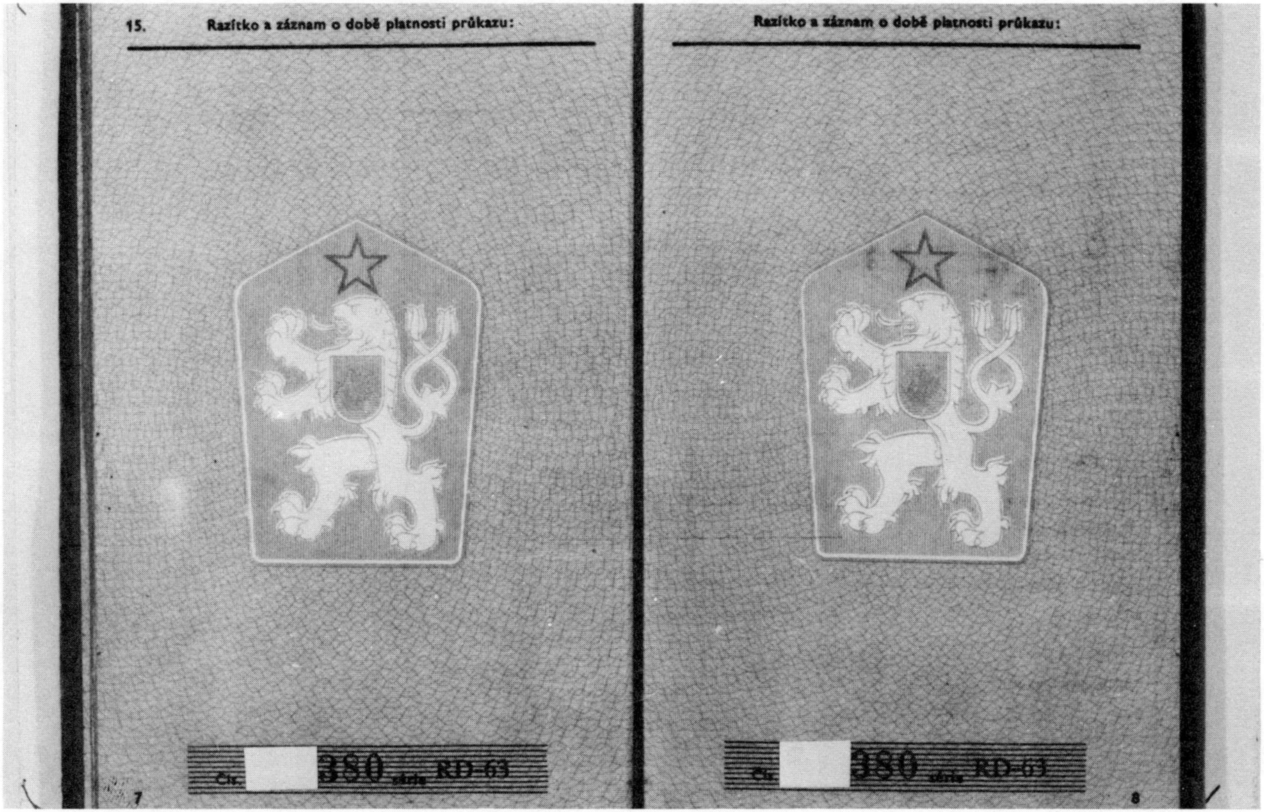

Figure 35 continued

Figure 36

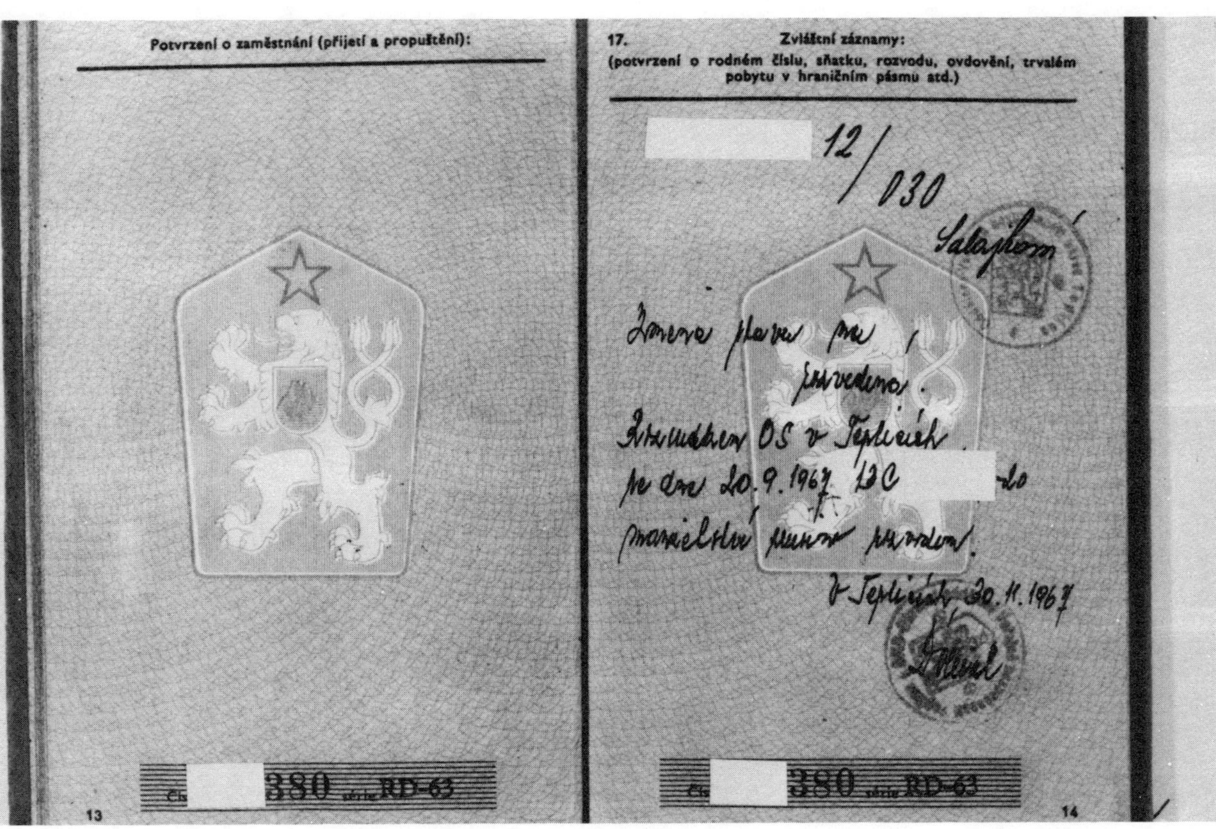

Figure 36 continued

Přihlášky a odhlášky pobytu:
Přihlášky a odhlášky pobytu:
Špindlerův Mlýn,
Přihlášen k přechodnému pobytu
1966
Přihlášen, (a) do:
Špindlerův Mlýn, okres Trutnov
Přihlášen k přechodnému pobytu
5 XII 1966
Přihlášen, (a) do:
380 RD-63
380 RD-63

Figure 37

POUČENÍ

1. Občanský průkaz je veřejná listina, kterou občan Československé socialistické republiky prokazuje svou totožnost, československé státní občanství, místo pobytu a jiné významné právní a evidenční skutečnosti zapsané v občanském průkazu. Zápisy v občanském průkazu nahrazují osvědčení o československém státním občanství, potvrzení o místě pobytu a ostatní veřejné listiny o skutečnostech, které jsou předmětem zápisu, a to v rozsahu uvedeném v občanském průkazu. Na vyzvání orgánů Veřejné bezpečnosti je každý povinen osobně se dostavit k výdeji občanského průkazu, popřípadě k doplnění zápisů v občanském průkazu.

2. Po převzetí občanského průkazu je držitel průkazu povinen bez průtahů předložit občanský průkaz:
   a) zaměstnavateli k zápisu údajů o pracovním (učebním) poměru, pokud je držitel průkazu v pracovním (učebním) poměru,
   b) orgánu okresního národního výboru k zápisu rodného čísla, pokud ve výjimečných případech tento zápis nemohl být proveden již při vydání občanského průkazu.

3. Držitel občanského průkazu je povinen dbát, aby základní údaje zapsané v občanském průkazu o jménu a příjmení, o stavu a o pobytu, jakož i údaje o zaměstnání, stále odpovídaly skutečnosti; za tím účelem je povinen:
   a) při změně příjmení nebo jména požádat oddělení VB o vydání nového občanského průkazu,
   b) při změně stavu (uzavření manželství, rozvodu manželství, ovdovění), pokud nedošlo ke změně příjmení nebo jména, předložit občanský průkaz s příslušným dokladem orgánu místního národního výboru k zápisu nastalé změny,
   c) při hlášení pobytu předložit občanský průkaz ohlašovně k zápisu údajů o pobytu; občanský průkaz, v němž ohlašovna provedla zápis o učiněném hlášení pobytu, předložit k nahlédnutí svému ubytovateli,
   d) při vzniku a ukončení pracovního (učebního) poměru předložit občanský průkaz zaměstnavateli k zápisu údajů o pracovním (učebním) poměru.

4. Vedlejší údaje se zapisují do občanského průkazu po jeho vydání pouze na žádost držitele průkazu; po předložení příslušného dokladu zapisuje
   a) orgán místního národního výboru – údaje o narození, osvojení nebo úmrtí dětí mladších 15 let,
   b) oddělení VB – údaje o sociálním postavení a vzdělání.

Čís. 380 série RD-63

5. Držitel občanského průkazu je dále povinen:
   a) chránit občanský průkaz před poškozením, zničením, ztrátou, odcizením nebo zneužitím nepovolanou osobou; v případě že tyto okolnosti nastaly, hlásit je neprodleně orgánům Veřejné bezpečnosti,
   b) prokazovat se občanským průkazem na vyzvání bezpečnostním a jiným orgánům k tomu zmocněným,
   c) požádat před uplynutím doby platnosti občanského průkazu orgány Veřejné bezpečnosti o prodloužení platnosti dosavadního občanského průkazu, po případě o vydání nového občanského průkazu,
   d) požádat neprodleně orgány Veřejné bezpečnosti o vydání nového občanského průkazu, ztratil-li dosavadní občanský průkaz svou průkazní moc.

6. Občanský průkaz ztrácí průkazní moc uplynutím doby platnosti v něm uvedené. Před uplynutím této doby ztrácí průkazní moc, jestliže
   a) byl poškozen, ztracen nebo odcizen,
   b) obsahuje nečitelné nebo nesprávné údaje nebo neoprávněně provedené změny, zápisy nebo opravy,
   c) držitel občanského průkazu změnil své příjmení nebo jméno nebo byla úředně provedena oprava matričního zápisu příjmení nebo jména,
   d) držitel občanského průkazu podstatně změnil svoji podobu.

7. Občanské průkazy nesmí být jejich držitelům odnímány při jejich vstupu do budov úřadů, podniků a závodů a nesmí být přijímány jako zástava. Občanský průkaz nesmí být přenášen do ciziny s výjimkou případů, kde je součástí cestovního dokladu.

8. Každý, kdo nalezne cizí občanský průkaz, je povinen odevzdat jej neprodleně orgánům Veřejné bezpečnosti. Občané, kteří nastoupili vojenskou činnou službu, jsou povinni odevzdat občanský průkaz příslušnému vojenskému orgánu.

9. Držitel průkazu nesmí provádět žádné zápisy, změny nebo úpravy v občanském průkazu.

10. Nesplnění nebo porušení některé ze shora uvedených povinností, zejména padělání, pozměnění, přenechání průkazu jiným osobám k použití nebo jako zástavy, nebo jiné zneužití občanského průkazu, je trestné.

MINISTERSTVO VNITRA
HLAVNÍ SPRÁVA VEŘEJNÉ BEZPEČNOSTI
V PRAZE

3000-61

Čís. 380 série RD-63

29   30

Figure 37 continued

ing of a two-letter prefix, a series number, then an Arabic number. This serial is printed on half of the pages, so that it appears always on each side of each unbound page spread.

The regulations and instructions for use of the SZEMELYI IGAZOLVANY occupy three full pages at the end.

The Hungarian document follows the Russian example of validating the bearer's photo by imprint of an embossed "dry seal" placed over the lower right corner.

Perhaps the most important and interesting feature of the exemplar illustrated here are the two border zone cachets on page eight which we mentioned earlier in our analysis of the Soviet PASPORT. These stamps with their ornamented borders and large numeral "2" at the right are so like the forbidden zone border residence cachets used in the USSR that a Soviet border guard would instantly recognize such an entry, even if he could not read the Hungarian text. And of course the converse would be true; a Hungarian would have no trouble identifying a border zone cachet in a Russian PASPORT.

The SZEMELYI IGAZOLVANY is illustrated in Figures 38-40.

PEOPLE'S REPUBLIC OF BULGARIA

Perhaps because the Bulgarian language is closest to Russian of all the countries in the Soviet block, and due to the similarities of alphabets used, it is not surprising that the Bulgarian citizen's basic identity booklet is most nearly like the Soviet PASPORT of all the Satellite documents. Even the title, LICHEN PASPORT ("Personal Identity Document"), is a close approximation of the Russian. Indeed, in only one respect does the LICHEN PASPORT differ sharply from the PASPORT, namely in having the bearer's photo fastened by means of metal grommets at the lower left and upper right corners (Figure 41). Also, like the Polish *DOWOD OSOBISTY* it has provision for a brief description of the bearer.

Otherwise the LICHEN PASPORT is pretty much a Bulgarian edition of the PASPORT. We see the familiar serial, with two-letter Cyrillic prefix and six-digit Arabic numeral, appearing on eight of the sixteen pages of the booklet.

Page five, containing columns for entering data on "children under 16 years," is an exact copy of the Russian page three. Residence registration shows one difference from the Soviet *propiska* system, in that one page is reserved for cachets showing the bearer's registration in the books of the "people's militia" (entered at time of issue of the document), while the subsequent four pages are intended for changes in residence and are entered by the "Address Service." Hiring cachets on the "place of work" pages are carbon copies of Soviet employment stamps. (See Figure 42.)

The brief "Obligations of the Bearer of the Lichen Pasport," on the inside back cover page, show the Soviet influence perhaps more inescapably than any other feature of the Satellite documents we have shown. (See Figure 43). Thus, Obligation 3 requires the bearer "Upon hiring and release from employment in an enterprise, establishment or organization—to present his LICHEN PASPORT to the appropriate offi-

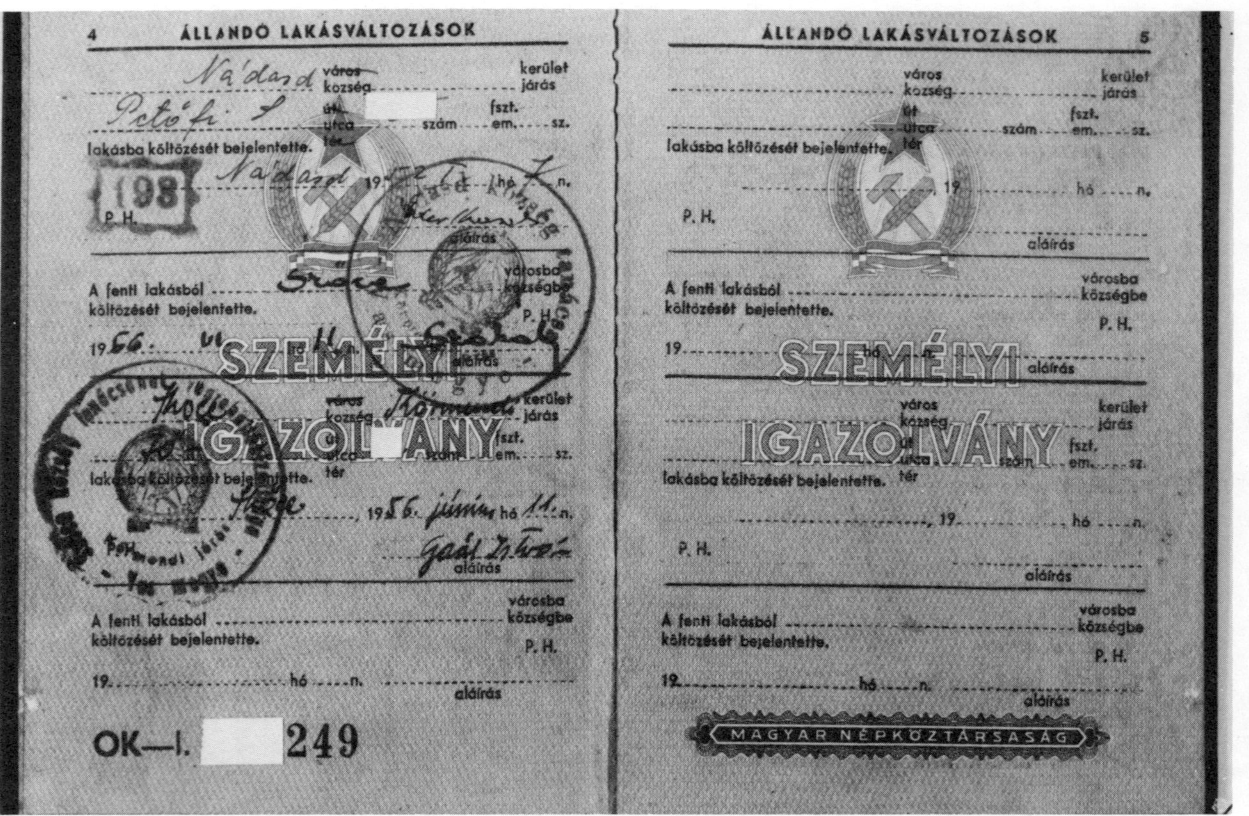

Figure 38

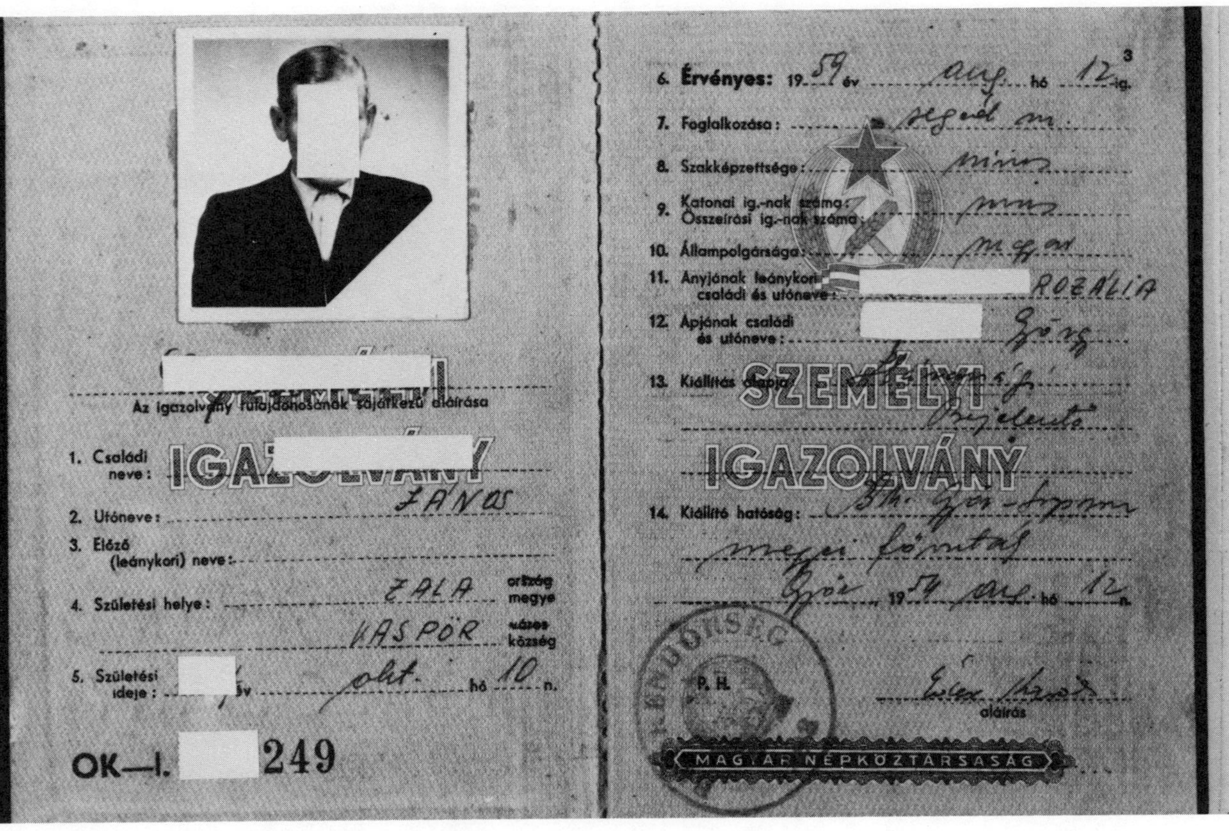

Figure 38 continued

Figure 39

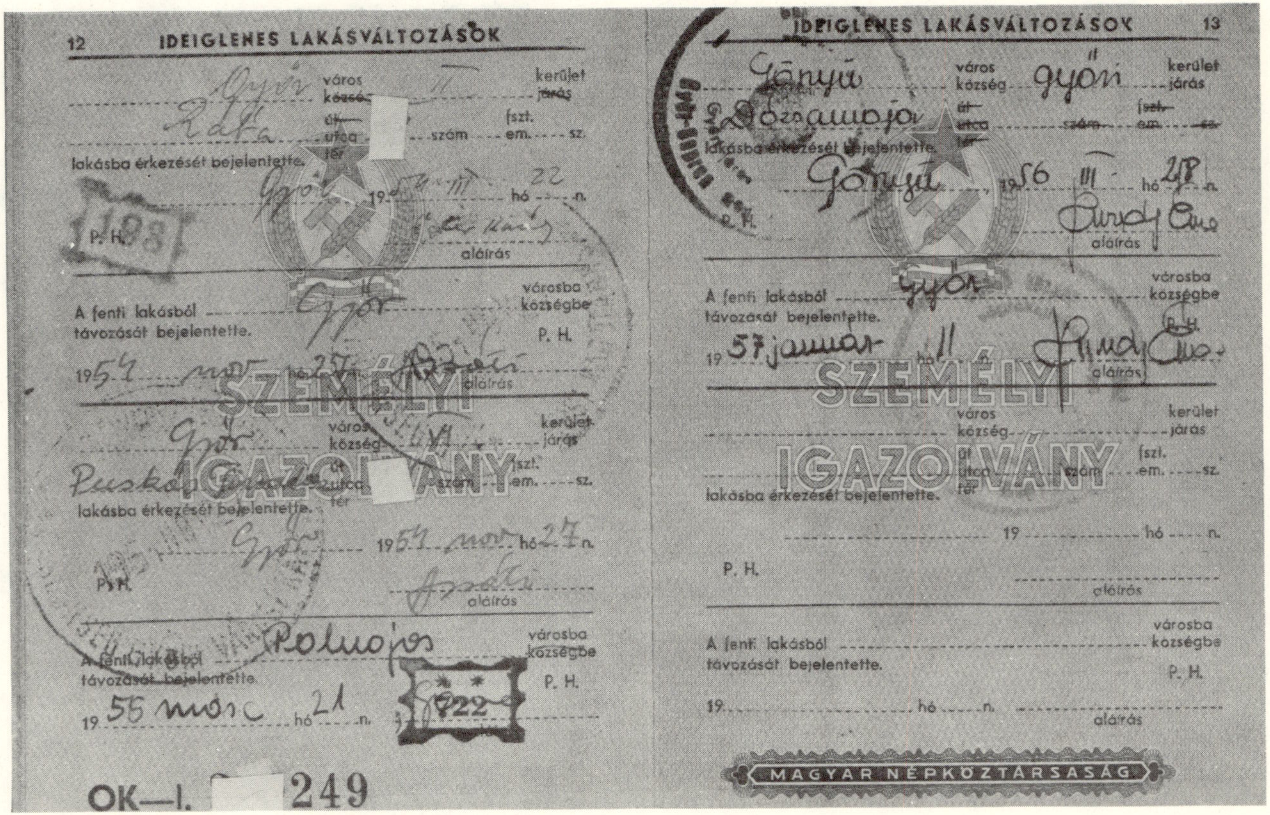

12 IDEIGLENES LAKÁSVÁLTOZÁSOK

város / község ... kerület / járás

út / utca / tér ... szám ... fszt. / em. ... sz.

lakásba érkezését bejelentette.

19... hó ... n.

P. H.

aláírás

A fenti lakásból távozását bejelentette. ... városba / községbe

P. H.

19... hó ... n. aláírás

város / község ... kerület / járás

út / utca / tér ... szám ... fszt. / em. ... sz.

lakásba érkezését bejelentette.

19... hó ... n.

P. H.

aláírás

A fenti lakásból távozását bejelentette. ... városba / községbe

P. H.

19... hó ... n.

OK—I. 249

IDEIGLENES LAKÁSVÁLTOZÁSOK 13

város / község ... kerület / járás

út / utca / tér ... szám ... fszt. / em. ... sz.

lakásba érkezését bejelentette.

19... hó ... n.

P. H.

aláírás

A fenti lakásból távozását bejelentette. ... városba / községbe

P. H.

19... hó ... n. aláírás

város / község ... kerület / járás

út / utca / tér ... szám ... fszt. / em. ... sz.

lakásba érkezését bejelentette.

19... hó ... n.

P. H.

aláírás

A fenti lakásból távozását bejelentette. ... városba / községbe

P. H.

19... hó ... n. aláírás

MAGYAR NÉPKÖZTÁRSASÁG

Figure 39 continued

Figure 40

Figure 40 continued

Figure 41

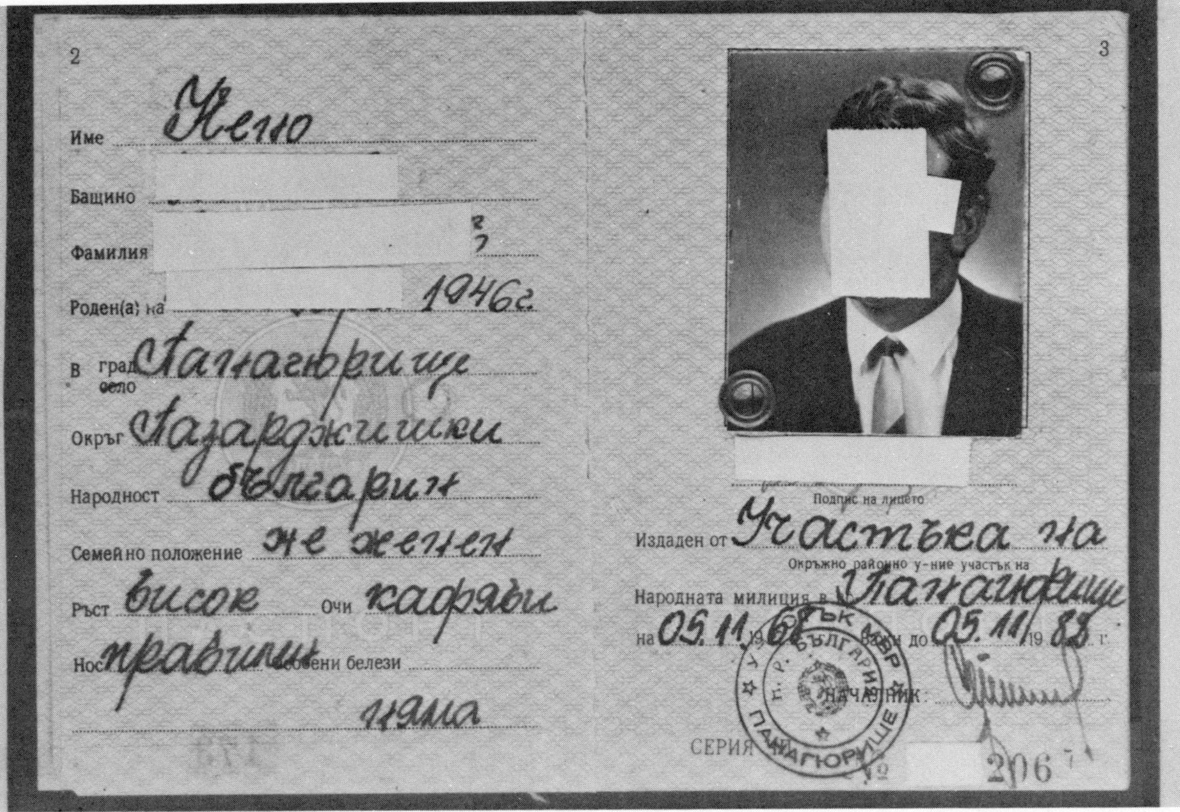

Figure 41 continued

ПРОМЕНИ В СЕМ. ПОЛОЖЕНИЕ
ДЕЦА ПОД 16 ГОДИНИ
Име
Дата на раждане
Местораждане
Заверка
СЕРИЯ. ЧП
№
206

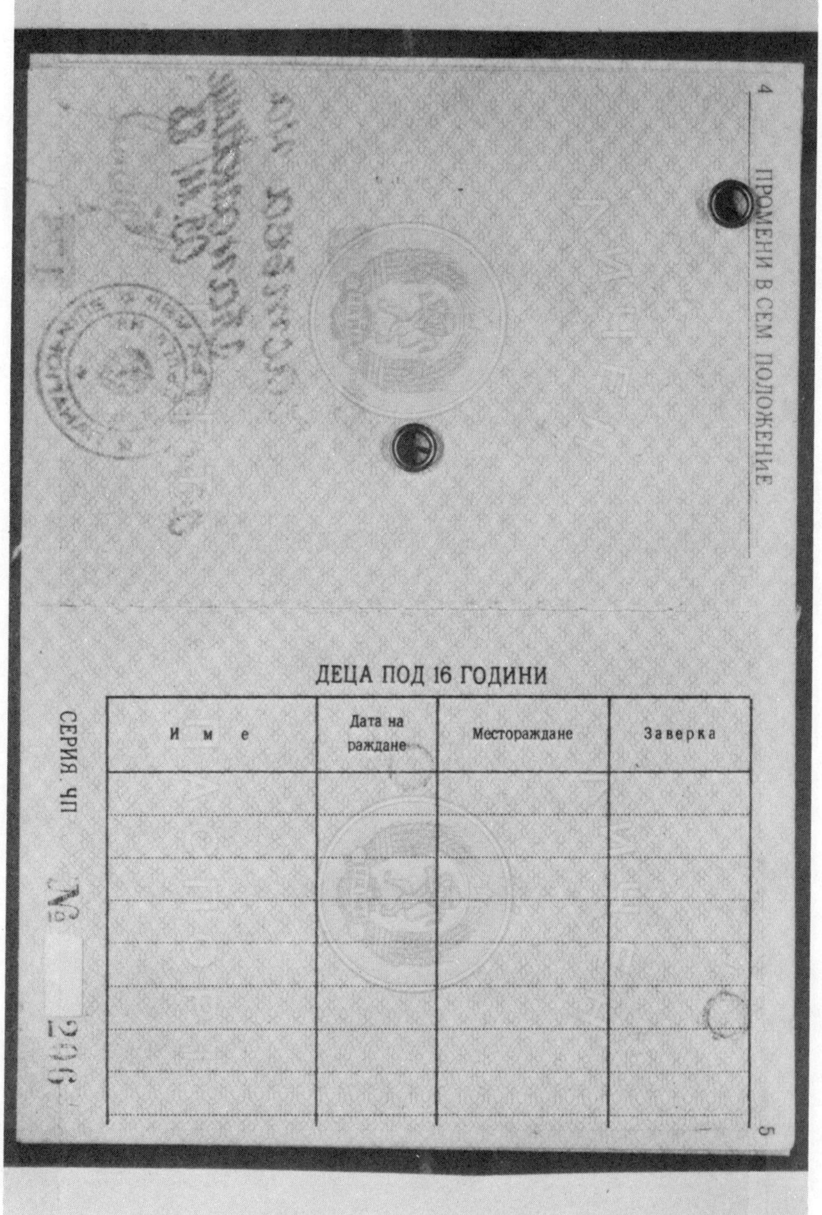

Figure 42

Figure 42 continued

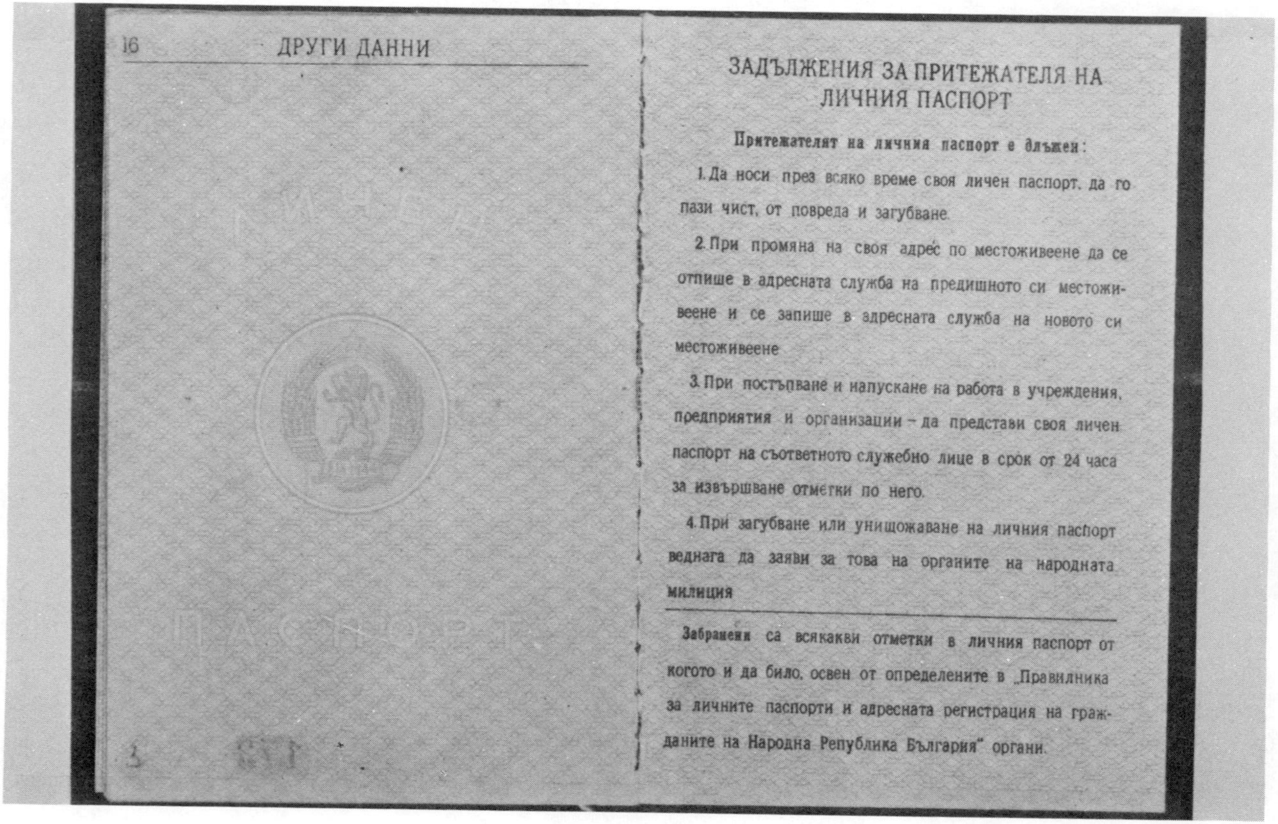

16   ДРУГИ ДАННИ

ЗАДЪЛЖЕНИЯ ЗА ПРИТЕЖАТЕЛЯ НА
ЛИЧНИЯ ПАСПОРТ

Притежателят на личния паспорт е длъжен:

1. Да носи през всяко време своя личен паспорт, да го пази чист, от повреда и загубване.

2. При промяна на своя адрес по местоживеене да се отпише в адресната служба на предишното си местоживеене и се запише в адресната служба на новото си местоживеене

3. При постъпване и напускане на работа в учреждения, предприятия и организации – да представи своя личен паспорт на съответното служебно лице в срок от 24 часа за извършване отметки по него.

4. При загубване или унищожаване на личния паспорт веднага да заяви за това на органите на народната милиция

Забранени са всякакви отметки в личния паспорт от когото и да било, освен от определените в „Правилника за личните паспорти и адресната регистрация на гражданите на Народна Република България" органи.

Figure 43

cial within 24 hours for entering notations concerning it." The Marxist-Leninist jargon used here is a direct borrowing from the Russian, particularly the identical words "*uchrezhdeniya, predpriyatiya i organizatsii,*" a tedious phrase through which we plodded so many times in dealing with the Soviet Work Booklet and the profsoyuz.

Our quick survey of Communist identity documents in use in Eastern Europe does not include an exemplar of a Rumanian identity booklet, and above all omits an illustration of one used in the German Democratic Republic. However, the reader may rest assured that such papers do exist and that they fulfill the same functions as those we have shown. The German version, a blue-covered booklet called *PERSONALAUSWEIS FUER DEUTSCH-ANGEHOERIGEN* ("Identity Document for German Nationals") has perhaps a less Soviet-like appearance than any of the others, but it provides the same stringent controls over the life of its holder as do the PASPORT and the other Satellite documents.

The document shown in Figure 45 shows that Soviet influence in personal documentation extends far beyond the confines of Europe. The booklet illustrated here is functionally more an equivalent of the Soviet VOYENNYY BILET than the PASPORT, but the Communist inspiration is unmistakable, from the great seal with its five-pointed star enclosed by sheaves of grain to the layout of pages. The document was carried by a member of the North Vietnamese armed forces. Its title may be translated roughly as "Proof of Identity Certificate."

The underprinting on each page of this Vietnamese document is also reminiscent of European Communist identity booklets, as is the page size and general for-

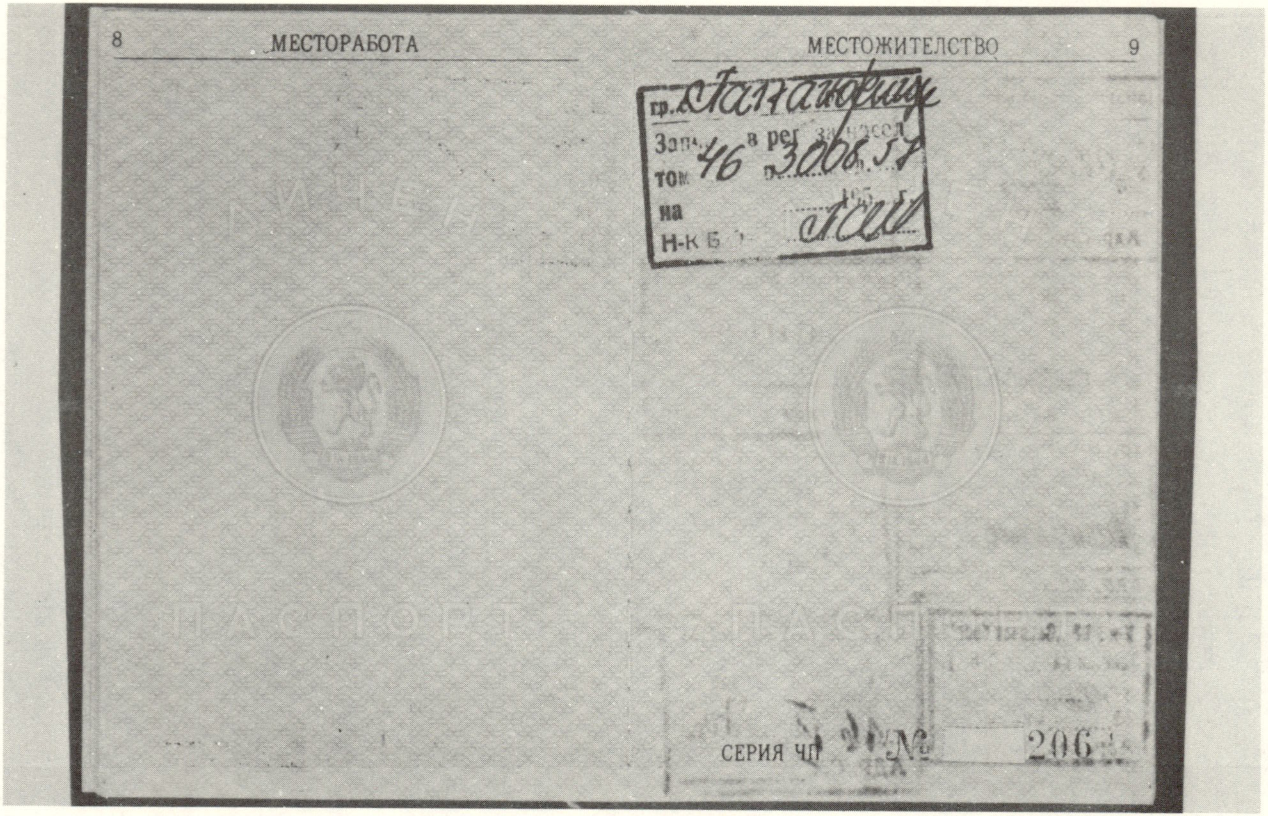

Figure 44

АДРЕСНА РЕГИСТРАЦИЯ

СЕРИЯ ЧП № 206

Figure 44 continued

QUÂN ĐỘI NHÂN DÂN VIỆT-NAM
NHÂN DẠNG
Cao 1 thước 57
dấu vết đặc biệt Có một bẹo
ở gò mai bên Phải
Họ tên
Cấp bậc Thượng úy
Nghị định số 088
Ngày 19. 11. 1958
Sinh ngày 1929
Nguyên quán
Triệu an Triệu phong Quảng trị
Ngày tháng 1 năm 1959
L. Bộ Trưởng Bộ Quốc Phòng
CHỦ NHIỆM Tổng Cục Cán Bộ
QUÂN ĐỘI NHÂN DÂN VIỆT NAM
TỔNG CỤC CÁN BỘ
BỘ TỔNG TƯ LỆNH
NGUYỄN-VĂN-VINH

Figure 45

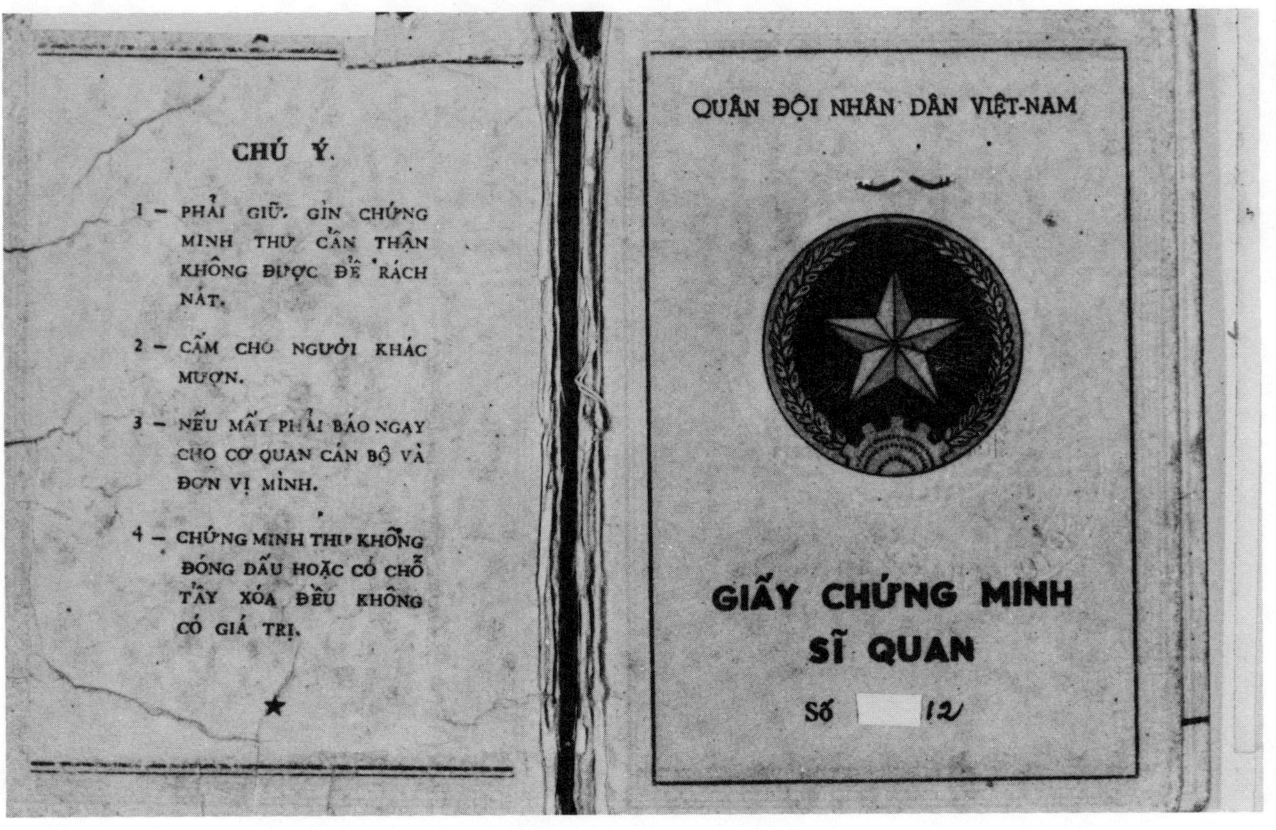

Figure 45 continued

THAY ĐỔI CHỨC VỤ

Chức vụ Trợ lý Thi đua
Đơn vị Sư đoàn 341
Cấp quyết định Sư đoàn 341
Số ngày 9.1958
Thủ Trưởng

Chức vụ Học viên
Đơn vị Học viện Quân chính
Cấp quyết định
Số ngày 30-7-1964
Thủ Trưởng

THAY ĐỔI CHỨC VỤ

Chức vụ
Đơn vị
Cấp quyết định
Số ngày
Thủ Trưởng

Chức vụ
Đơn vị
Cấp quyết định
Số ngày
Thủ Trưởng

Figure 46

Figure 46 continued

mat. The text printing provides for such data as name, physical description, rank or position, issue date, basis of issue, changes in work assignment, changes in status, and issuance of weapons. The first text page contains instructions, including the requirement that the document be carried on the person. Figure 46 appears to contain entries similar to the military roll registration found in the Soviet VOYENNY BILET.

From the document exemplars illustrated in this Section it seems evident that many Communist countries which look to the Soviet Union for leadership in ideology accept also the dictates of that "motherland" in the matter of absolute State control over the individual. The countries of Eastern Europe may display some measure of independence in some areas of their national life, but underlying these differences lies a hard core of Soviet mastery of its sphere of influence. At the core, where the real power structure is concerned, the police and the military in the satellite states are in effect still just auxiliaries of the MVD, KGB and the Red Army. We can glimpse in this a uniformity of identity documentation and registration procedures which exists throughout the Communist Bloc, varying only because of the particular requirements of local conditions. Given the indispensability of such control measures if Communist order in society is to be preserved, we must assume that any attempt by one of these countries to liberalize fundamentally these control institutions would certainly meet with the kind of uncompromising opposition with which the Soviet Union has answered challenges to that Communist order in the past, as in the Hungarian and Czech uprisings. The stifling of Polish freedom initiatives is eloquent testimony to the correctness of this belief.

BIBLIOGRAPHY

Bol'shaya Sovetskaya Entsiklopediya *(Great Russian Encyclopedia)*, 1st edition, Moscow.

Conquest, Robert. 1968. *The Soviet Police System.* New York: Praeger.

‾‾‾‾‾ 1967. *Industrial Workers in the USSR.* New York & Washington: Praeger.

Profsoyuzy SSSR (Trade Unions of the USSR). Moscow, 1974

Rybal'chenko, R.K. Pasportnaya sistema v SSSR (Passport system in the USSR), Kiev, "Vishcha shkola", 1977.

Zapis' aktov grazhdanskogo sostoyaniya (Registry of civil vital statistics), Ministry of Justice RSFSR, State Printing House for Juridical Literature, Moscow 1961.

Ugolovnyy kodeks RSFSR (Criminal Code of the RSFSR) Official text, Moscow, 1966.

Studenikin, S.S., Vlasov, V.A. & I.I. Yevtikhiyev. Sovetskoye administrativnoye pravo (Soviet Administrative Law), State Publishing House for Juridical Literature, Moscow, 1950.

INDEX